This book is a must-read. The quotati[ons]
in many fields are priceless. The reader will meet himself
or herself several times in this book, and each meeting will
leave the reader a better person who understands others
better. Regardless of whether you are an employer or
employee, military or civilian, you will be a better person
after applying the insights in this book, and consequently,
you'll better perform the job with which you have
been entrusted.

LT. JIM DOWNING, author of *The Other Side of Infamy*

As a pastor who wants to equip the men in my church to
better serve their God, Christ's church, their families, and
our community, I'm so grateful for this book and Charles
Causey's practical, engaging, and scriptural call for men
to live congruent lives—lives where our words and deeds
truly please our Lord.

ARRON CHAMBERS, pastor and author, *Eats with Sinners: Loving
like Jesus*

Our own fathers or grandfathers may not have needed this
book. But we do. I do. We live in an age of spin. Talking
a good game matters more than living a good life, and
the art of persuasion is more valued than plain speech
and honest action. Charles Causey steps into the muddle
and issues a clear call for men to say what we mean,
mean what we say, and do what we promise. It's too bad
we need this reminder. But it's so good that it comes in

this form—so clear, so simple, so sane, so direct. I have a mental list of several men who need this book. At the top of the list is my own name.

MARK BUCHANAN, bestselling writer and professor of pastoral theology, Ambrose University

Weaving stories with practical God-honoring advice, Charles Causey gives us a solid study on why words and deeds are both essential in building lives that matter.

MAJOR GENERAL USAR (RETIRED) DANIEL YORK, founder and director, First Cause

We often have a false dichotomy between the importance of actions and words. The reality is that it is extremely important for Christian men to live out their own discipleship in a way that encompasses both the content of their words and the quality of their actions. Charles Causey does a wonderful job helping us identify the nature of our own discipleship as we speak and live while giving us practical tools to grow into the fullness of Jesus Christ.

REV. DR. DANA S. ALLIN, synod executive of ECO, a Covenant Order of Evangelical Presbyterians

WORDS AND DEEDS

BECOMING
A MAN OF
COURAGEOUS
INTEGRITY

CHARLES CAUSEY

A NavPress resource published in alliance
with Tyndale House Publishers, Inc.

NAVPRESS⬤®

NavPress is the publishing ministry of The Navigators, an international Christian organization and leader in personal spiritual development. NavPress is committed to helping people grow spiritually and enjoy lives of meaning and hope through personal and group resources that are biblically rooted, culturally relevant, and highly practical.

For more information, visit www.NavPress.com.

The Team:

Don Pape, Publisher

David Zimmerman, Acquisitions Editor

Elizabeth Symm, Copy Editor

Mark Anthony Lane II, Designer

Published in association with the Steve Laube Agency, 24 W. Camelback Rd. A-635, Phoenix, AZ 85013.

Cataloging-in-Publication Data is available.

ISBN 978-1-63146-804-9

Printed in the United States of America

24	23	22	21	20	19	18
7	6	5	4	3	2	1

For Nick and Isaiah

He which hath no stomach to this fight,
Let him depart; his passport shall be made,
And crowns for convoy put into his purse.
We would not die in that man's company
That fears his fellowship to die with us.

SHAKESPEARE, *HENRY V*

CONTENTS

INTRODUCTION

You are about to embark upon a great crusade.

JUNE 5, 1944. Despite the cool breeze and light mist, the twenty-thousand-plus men of the 82nd and 101st Airborne Divisions prepared for their predawn airdrop behind enemy lines at Normandy. They had just received word the mission was a "go."

The tarmac at Greenham Common airfield was filled with nervous bodies and piles of equipment waiting to be loaded onto aircraft. Paratroopers were briefed by their jumpmasters. Chaplains held impromptu worship services with clusters of men. Suddenly, a path cleared for a high-ranking officer making his way through the crowds of men.

General Dwight D. Eisenhower left his forward command post, a place called Southwick House near Portsmouth, to meet with US paratroopers who were receiving last-minute pre-invasion instructions. General Eisenhower would visit every division preparing for Operation Overlord that day, but he wanted to start with his airborne units; in a few hours, they would depart—the first division to cross the channel and drop behind Utah Beach. The Supreme Allied Commander had been informed that more than 50 percent of the paratroopers and 70 percent of those in gliders would die before hitting the ground, so the general decided to visit them first to offer words of encouragement.

With England's fast-moving gray skies in the background, the four-star commander walked among the troops, shook their hands, and spoke to them. With more than one hundred thousand men preparing to cross the channel for the invasion of France, this would be the largest amphibious assault ever attempted. Eisenhower hoped his words would prepare the men for battle, give them courage, and make them defiant against all odds. The following is his pre-invasion battle order:

Soldiers, Sailors and Airmen of the Allied
Expeditionary Force!

You are about to embark upon the Great
Crusade, toward which we have striven these many
months. The eyes of the world are upon you.
The hopes and prayers of liberty-loving people
everywhere march with you. In company with our
brave Allies and brothers-in-arms on other Fronts,
you will bring about the destruction of the German
war machine, the elimination of Nazi tyranny over
the oppressed peoples of Europe, and security for
ourselves in a free world.

Your task will not be an easy one. Your enemy is
well trained, well equipped and battle-hardened. He
will fight savagely.

But this is the year 1944! Much has happened since the Nazi triumphs of 1940–41. The United Nations have inflicted upon the Germans great defeats, in open battle, man-to-man. Our air offensive has seriously reduced their strength in the air and their capacity to wage war on the ground. Our Home Fronts have given us an overwhelming superiority in weapons and munitions of war, and placed at our disposal great reserves of trained fighting men. The tide has turned! The free men of the world are marching together to Victory!

I have full confidence in your courage, devotion to duty and skill in battle.

We will accept nothing less than full Victory!

Good Luck! And let us all beseech the blessing of Almighty God upon this great and noble undertaking.[1]

The men were thankful for his visit, however brief, and were more resolved than ever to embark on their nighttime journey to attack the Germans.

* * * *

Most men inherently know the importance of deeds. Without great deeds of conquest, battles would never be won. While the US Army and other Allied forces advanced through western Europe, the US Marines and the US Navy were battling to win the island of Iwo Jima.

However, words are important too. Soldiers will die. It

is the nature of war. But well-chosen words delivered with all due sobriety can help remind and encourage those same soldiers that they and their comrades will die with meaning, that they will not die in vain. Leaders must exhort warriors to fight and must explain the cause that puts their lives in jeopardy. Throughout history, decisive battle speeches given by men like Napoleon and Eisenhower were just as vital as deeds of conquest in moving men into action.

The same is true within our families, our careers, and our communities: Our deeds as men are absolutely critical to our success, and so are our words. Even more importantly, there needs to be synthesis between the two. We cannot simply tell our children to do the right thing; they must see us doing good deeds, and they must be persuaded with our good words. We cannot only be faithful in deeds to our spouses or bosses; they need us to verbally engage with them, and they need us to be men of our word. We have to perform good deeds to accomplish goals, but it is also necessary to influence others positively with our good words.

Conversely, we may tell our children to do the right thing, but if they see us doing the wrong thing, our words are meaningless. At the same time, if we do the right thing in view of our children without drawing their attention to the value of right action and the reasons for acting rightly, our children can easily learn the wrong lessons—if they even notice our actions.

It is possible to spend a significant part of our lives without living intentionally, without thinking about the synthesis of our words and deeds. Sometimes we need a course correction.

The goal of this book is not only to develop a greater self-awareness among men but also to apply this knowledge for life change. Both words *and* deeds are important. Their alignment is important too, for to the extent that our words and deeds are not aligned (and, importantly, pointed toward the good), our lives will lack personal meaning and broader impact.

The most influential men in history were strong and mighty in both words and deeds. Martin Luther King Jr. is remembered for his speeches, but he rose to national prominence for his contribution to the civil rights movement. Theodore Roosevelt was a master of the "bully pulpit," using the force of his words to sway the mood and will of a nation, but he is remembered even more for his military exploits and international adventures. In the Gospel of Luke (24:19), Jesus was said to be mighty in both words and deeds. Moses is another example; he spoke to the people of Israel and showed them incredible examples of God's power. Both words and deeds are necessary for an exemplary life, and this book speaks about their integration—closing the gap between the men we are and the men we want to be.

Think about the men and women in your life who influenced you the most. What do you notice about their words and actions? Were they people of integrity?

Here are some of the questions I ask and answer in this book:

- How does a man appear to others when he is mostly talk and no action?

- What about a man with all deeds and few words?
- Which man are you?
- How do others see you?
- Is there a gap between the man you portray to others and the man you actually are?

Words and Deeds was written to help men identify whether there is integrity between their words and actions, and—if not—to give them tools for alignment. Men cannot embark on this kind of change alone, however; men need other men to keep them accountable and God to give them strength. I have attached a six-week study guide with individual and small group questions at the end of this book so men can make those vital connections. I encourage every man reading *Words and Deeds* to form a small group and discuss these concepts with other men. Also, you will have the opportunity for three people to assess you via an online diagnostic so you can compare your own results with what they say of your words and deeds. This experience should lead to a greater self-understanding and reveal whether the man you believe you are is the same man that others are experiencing.

Finally, I understand that something is always lost between an author's intent and a reader's perception of that intent, and this book will prove no exception. Not everyone who reads *Words and Deeds* will feel compelled to partake in the necessary alignment work to experience lasting life change. But I trust that this short book *will* make every man who reads it pause to consider the critical continuum between his words and actions, and in so doing, move one step closer to who the Master created him to be. The material in this book changed my life, and I pray it will change yours, too.

CHAPTER 1

THE MAN IN THE ARENA

Just pray that I shall be adequate.

WHEN I WAS A YOUNG MAN, my army chaplain father told me a true story about 672 men who perished in the middle of the night during World War II. On January 23, 1943, the SS *Dorchester* departed New York City harbor, heading east across the icy North Atlantic with more than nine hundred servicemen on board.[1] Most were newly trained American soldiers on their way to Europe to serve in the war. Four of these men—Methodist minister Rev. George Fox, Rabbi Alexander Goode, Reformed Church minister Rev. Clark Poling, and Roman Catholic priest Father John Washington—were recently commissioned army chaplains who worked hard to keep up the morale of the troops in a ship claustrophobically packed to capacity.

Close to one o'clock on the morning of February 3, a German submarine spotted the *Dorchester* 150 miles from the coast of Greenland and fired three torpedoes toward its middle. One of the torpedoes struck the starboard side far below the waterline, causing irreparable damage and immediately killing scores of men. The entire vessel would sink to the bottom of the Atlantic within thirty minutes. The captain gave the order to abandon ship. In the pandemonium that followed, men searched for life jackets and rafts in the dark, desperately trying to save their lives.

The four chaplains, who had organized a variety show in the enlisted men's galley earlier that evening, quickly went into action, quietly and calmly guiding men in the blackened ship. They led their fellow soldiers to where they could evacuate the vessel, opened a deck locker filled with extra life jackets, and distributed them to the panicked soldiers. They gave up their gloves and hats; eventually, when there were no more life jackets, the four chaplains took off their own vests and made others put them on. Witnesses such as Sergeant Kenzel Linaweaver[2] of the 304th Infantry and Robert C. Williams recounted that it was the most astonishing act of courage they ever saw. Two men already floating in the oily water, Sergeant Thomas Myers and Private First Class John O'Brien, remembered hearing screams of panic from the men still on board, followed by words of courage and hope from the chaplains. At last glimpse, the four chaplains were seen arm in arm, singing and praying together as the *Dorchester* slipped under water.

My father, Calvin Causey, knew Clark's father, Dan Poling, personally. Once, on a walk together, Poling explained to my father that he had spoken to Clark a few days before the *Dorchester* set sail. The young army lieutenant told his father, "Please do not pray for my safe return; that wouldn't be fair. Just pray that I shall be adequate." My own father choked up before he could finish the story. "The four chaplains were more than adequate," he said softly. "They did their duty."

* * * *

What would inspire men to take off their life jackets, give them to other men, and go down with the ship? It is obvious that, in a very short time, the four chaplains had developed a very robust identity as servants of God. That identity and their calling to serve shaped them more than the very natural instinct of self-preservation. No doubt, not all four men had the same courage that night, but witnessing each other's bravery and fortitude bound them together in a united mission to serve their fellow soldiers.

As men, our main purpose in life radiates around taking care of other people: our immediate families, our work associates, the communities we are part of, our aging parents. Like the four army chaplains, we are called to serve others and lead by example, to occupy our space and not shrink back from it. Trust comes from delivering on our promises and commitments. When men speak encouraging words to others and perform deeds of valor, they become everything the Master made them to be, and they encourage other men to do the same.

King David declared in Psalm 19:13-14, "Keep back Your servant from presumptuous sins. . . . Let the words of my mouth and the meditation of my heart be acceptable in Your sight." David knew both his words and his deeds were evident to God, and he wanted them to be pleasing to Him.

Here is the three-point premise of this book:

- The words we say as men are very important.
- The deeds we do as men are equally vital.
- Aligning our words and deeds is crucial for an impactful life.

Deeds

So what is meant by *words* and *deeds*? Starting with *deeds*, most men fundamentally comprehend that deeds are important. But what is a deed? A deed is an *intentional action*. In the context of this book, a deed is something beneficial, a good work, a kind act, an aid rendered. It is an act that *accomplishes* something in life, and there are many quotes about being a man of deeds.[3] In fact, there is an entire nursery rhyme that denigrates words that are not complemented by deeds.

A MAN OF WORDS AND NOT OF DEEDS

A man of words and not of deeds
Is like a garden full of weeds
And when the weeds begin to grow
It's like a garden full of snow
And when the snow begins to fall

It's like a bird upon the wall
And when the bird away does fly
It's like an eagle in the sky
And when the sky begins to roar
It's like a lion at the door
And when the door begins to crack
It's like a stick across your back
And when your back begins to smart
It's like a penknife in your heart
And when your heart begins to bleed
You're dead, and dead, and dead indeed.[4]

ANONYMOUS

The reasons for doing deeds are self-evident. In order to live a good life, it is necessary to do good deeds for others. The reason many men—Moses, King David, Jesus, Constantine, Charlemagne, Gutenberg, Michelangelo, Mozart, George Washington, and Thomas Edison, to name a few—are called great is because they accomplished great deeds. These men did more than the average man; they put their lives to work for other people.

I often think about the four chaplains from the beginning story. These men positively impacted other human lives with their words, deeds, and example. It did not take an entire lifetime for them to accomplish something great; they took a step of faith in a harrowing moment and now will forever be enshrined in the annals of brave deeds. Though many of us may never know the extent of our actions while living here on earth, we must realize that simple steps of faith and courage on a daily basis can echo in eternity and imprint on lives we will never meet.

Here is an excerpt of a speech given by President Theodore Roosevelt, entitled "Citizenship in a Republic":

> It is not the critic who counts; not the man who points out how the strong man stumbles or where the doer of deeds could have done them better. The credit belongs to the man who is actually in the arena, whose face is marred by dust and sweat and blood; who strives valiantly; who errs, who comes short again and again, because there is no effort without error and shortcoming; but who does actually strive to do the deeds; who knows great enthusiasms, the great devotions; who spends himself in a worthy cause; who at the best knows in the end the triumph of high achievement, and who at the worst, if he fails, at least fails while daring greatly, so that his place shall never be with those cold and timid souls who neither know victory nor defeat.[5]

Do you ever feel like the man in the arena? With a face marred by dust and sweat and blood? Do you sometimes feel alone, fighting a battle no one else can see? So many people remain outside the arena, easily able to point out how the strong man stumbles and where he could have performed better. It is much more comfortable outside the arena. It is safer where there is no sacrifice. However, men outside the arena will never fully experience victory or defeat. They will not know the deepest joys and pains in life. One thing history teaches us is that there are no great accomplishments without great effort. Thus, deeds are important for a successful life.

Words

Have you ever heard someone say to you, "Put in a good word for me"? What they mean is to build them up and elevate them somehow in another person's eyes. What is a good word? A good word is speech or writing that is desirable, approving, or morally right. It is normally used to encourage someone or to motivate them to action. When Abraham Lincoln warned that "a house divided against itself cannot stand," he was not only offering his own good words—he was drawing on good words from the Bible to mark a moment and direct the course of history. When Ronald Reagan told Mikhail Gorbachev to "tear down this wall," he invested a simple phrase—four syllables in four words—with the weight of history and the force of moral courage.

Words are incredibly powerful and can be a force for good or for harm. As many of us men realize, the old preschool saying "Sticks and stones can break my bones, but words will never hurt me" is not true. Words can hurt people deeply and have a lasting effect.

One problem we face is that we live in a society where a man's word does not have much value anymore. A friend of mine told me that when her grandfather was a young man purchasing part of a neighbor's farm, the two only shook hands and the farmer said, "Your word is better than a piece of paper." Now, a simple handshake will not do.

When we make promises to one another, we often "give our word" and offer assurances that "our word is our bond." The other person decides whether to "take us at our word." We might reinforce our position by offering, "Don't take *my* word for it" and refer them to some independent source of verification. In each case, "my word" is an allusion to "my character," an implicit acknowledgment that the words we say have real meaning; our character can in fact be judged by them. But the sad flow of history has meant that one person's word—a simple *yes* or *no*—is no longer supported by confidence in his character. Instead of "my word," we resort to pages and pages of words—not our words but the words of our lawyers, densely written, highly technical legal language packed with caveats and conditions and exit clauses. This is what happens when we fail to follow through on what we say.

Societal promises are broken repeatedly, even when a man gives his word. Marriage vows are an example of this duplicity: On average, they are only kept half the time. Political promises are kept even less often than that. A recent report[6] from Barna, a market research group, highlights this mismatch by revealing there are 114 million adults in America who have nothing to do with church, yet 41 percent—46 million—of these people say that their religious faith is very important in their lives today. How is this possible?

The words we say as men are paramount. I could even argue that they are critical to sustaining life. Sometimes, the mere act of saying words has a beneficial result. Take, for instance, Franklin Delano Roosevelt's assurance to the nation that "the only thing we have to fear is fear itself." This is an example of words strengthening an entire society—not a preamble to a policy but a moral, rhetorical declaration. Words are more important than we can ever imagine: Good words can help win wars, help conquer racism, allocate life-saving funds, and strengthen churches, marriages, friendships, communities, and human lives.

In warfare, words are used not merely as persuasive pre-battle speeches, as mentioned in the introduction; words are used throughout the day, in every battle, for the entire war. Battle plans are communicated to subordinate commanders ahead of time in an operations order; fragmentary orders are given by military leaders to provide a change of plans at decisive points during the battle; speeches are given by commanders after the battle; and combat experiences are retold by soldiers when they return home. Words of strategy are written in regulations, field manuals, and the magazines soldiers read in order to learn their military occupational specialty. Written war plans are encoded via secret messages, the Internet, walkie-talkies, and military radios. All of these methods effectively utilize words to help win a battle.

In marriage, words are used to win a mate, commit to her in the marriage ceremony, and support and encourage her throughout the relationship. As the years progress, words are used to continually woo a wife and make her feel like the girl from that first date.

In a family, words are used to teach children manners and coax them to eat their vegetables, do their homework, or mow the lawn. Words are also used to speak truth into people's lives, expressing their worth to you and to God. Encouraging words give elderly parents satisfaction in their parenting and sometimes hope for a future. Words also encourage siblings who are down on their luck to continue to run the race and fight the good fight.

Another area where intentional word usage is paramount is our careers, where words are utilized in numerous ways: to communicate the organizational mission, to hire and fire, to sustain a labor force, and to market and exchange goods and services. In our communities, we use words to greet neighbors, hire babysitters, organize car pools, and care for neighbors. In churches, exhortatory words are preached in sermons, delivered by teachers and leaders, and conveyed in small groups and the church nursery. Also, God's spoken Word is the foundation of Christian theology. Jesus is introduced as "the Word" who "was with God, and . . . was God" (John 1:1). In the book of Revelation, "His name is called The Word of God" (19:13).

Conversely, the lack of good words can influence a society negatively: Adolf Hitler's speeches and writings implicated an entire country in racist, imperialist, genocidal practices; the legendary royal snub "Let them eat cake" fueled the fires of revolution in France; a cult leader's self-promoting words induced nearly a thousand followers to drink poison.[7]

Good words are absolutely vital to function in society. We cannot merely be men of deeds and not words. Words are necessary. Words can be used for great good. We can protect someone from tripping over an obstacle, save a marriage, shield a child from an accident, or save a life by offering hopeful words. In my work as an army chaplain, sometimes a soldier whom I've never met will come into my office with tear-filled eyes, and the words I communicate to him or her in the next moments are critical. The words we men say to our spouses, our bosses, our work colleagues, our friends, and our neighbors are imperative to sustain our relationships here on planet Earth. Therefore, even though there may not be nursery rhymes elevating words over deeds, words are also crucial for a successful life.

*   *   *   *

A Presbyterian preacher by the name of Nathaniel Randolph Snowden captured an event in his diary of remembrances, and it remains a testament of history to this day.[8] In the document, Rev. Snowden describes meeting a man by the name of Isaac Potts who lived and worked at Valley Forge in the late 1770s. They shared a carriage, and Potts told Snowden about running into George Washington during the Revolutionary War.

Isaac Potts, a British sympathizer, owned and operated a gristmill at Valley Forge during the time of the Continental Army encampment. Potts told Snowden that on a snowy day in 1777, he was walking through the woods at Valley Forge and heard someone deep in prayer, beseeching God for the success of the Continental Army and the American cause. When he walked closer, he noticed a lone man, and that man was none other than General George Washington. When Potts returned home, he told his wife that America could prevail. Then he immediately changed his loyalties, became a patriot, and did whatever he could to support the colonists.

Think of the impact of George Washington's prayer at Valley Forge. It not only caused Isaac Potts to shift from British Loyalist to American Patriot, but it might have also influenced his neighbors, family, church, town—and thus the entire war. Reflect also on the heroic actions of George Washington during the Revolutionary War. General Washington utilized both words and deeds to win the war. His prayers and letters to Congress urging them for more resources are testaments of his use of words; his leadership and involvement in battles against the British are testaments of his use of deeds. Words and deeds are absolutely indispensable to life. And the two must be aligned.

> Whatever you do, whether in word and deed, do it all in the name of the Lord Jesus, giving thanks to God the Father through him.
>
> COLOSSIANS 3:17, NIV

CHAPTER 2

INTEGRITY DEFINED

I shall return.

WHEN I WALK THROUGH THE PENTAGON, I enjoy reading about the history of the military in the many displays throughout the seventeen miles of corridors in the 6.6-million-square-foot building. In one hallway on the third floor, there is a display for a famous army general. His seven Silver Stars, two Purple Hearts, and three Distinguished Service Crosses are all on display, as well as the Medals of Honor earned by him and his Civil War father. The man is General Douglas MacArthur.

In 1941, the Japanese army invaded the Philippines. In the ensuing months, nearly twenty-five thousand American military personnel would be killed, and the high commander was General Douglas MacArthur. MacArthur had retired from the US Army in 1937 after serving as the Army Chief of Staff. During the summer of 1941, he was recalled to active duty by President Roosevelt and sent to the Philippines as the Commander of US Army Forces in the Far East. In 1942, as Japan stormed the island of Luzon, Manila eventually fell and the US surrendered more than seventy-five thousand troops on the Bataan Peninsula—men who would endure the Bataan Death March to prison camps.

MacArthur himself had moved his headquarters to the island of Corregidor in Manila Bay. Ordered to leave the Philippines by President Roosevelt, MacArthur, his family, and his staff departed Corregidor on the night of March 12, 1942. Choosing not to take the safer option of a submarine, MacArthur and his crew embarked on patrol torpedo boats and for two days endured the stormy seas and risked Japanese warships. Once General MacArthur arrived at an Allied air base, he was flown on a B-17 bomber to Melbourne, Australia, where he decided to write a speech to encourage the many prisoners and Filipino citizens. Deeply disappointed and personally horrified by leaving the Philippines to the Japanese, MacArthur gave an address that contained these words: "I came through and I shall return!"

After battling for two years to retake New Guinea, in October 1944, MacArthur once again entered Philippine waters on a patrol torpedo boat and waded ashore in knee-deep water. MacArthur had finally returned, with a strong Allied force behind him. He declared, "To the people of the Philippines: I have returned. By the grace of Almighty God our forces stand again on Philippine soil—soil consecrated in the blood of our two peoples."[1]

MacArthur's words matched his deeds. It took two and a half years, but MacArthur returned and rescued the people he left behind. It is a great story of integrity. It is a reflection of the superior story of Christ, who said He would rise again and then did.

* * * *

Integrity means continuity. The word itself comes from the Latin word *integer*, meaning "entire," or "whole." It means coherence, unity, soundness. With integrity, things are not ambiguous. There is clarity, morally or otherwise. To have integrity means to have an absence of duplicity. In ethics, it means to have consistency of character or uncorrupted virtue. A man of integrity has his words and deeds *integrated*, with no sunlight in between the two.

A distinction: *Ethics* means that someone has a set of moral principles by which to live. It is what a man believes and tells others that he believes. *Morality*, though similar to ethics, is concerned with behavior. To have morality means one distinguishes between good and bad behavior and chooses the former. In short, a man's ethics are the rules to which he ascribes; his morals are how he lives and the deeds he does. To have integrity means a man's ethics and moral living are integrated, and this will always put him on the high road, but this is not the same with some of the other virtues.

For instance, the words *respect*, *duty*, and *loyalty* do not hold a moral component to them, and in a way, they presuppose an ethical blindness. Being loyal to people or institutions is great—until they veer off course. "My honor is loyalty" was the motto of the *Schutzstaffel*, Hitler's paramilitary organization during his reign over Germany. Out of loyalty to Hitler and as an ironic matter of "honor," Schutzstaffel soldiers committed war crimes and human atrocities, materially participating in the Holocaust. Loyalty is great, but it's morally neutral—which means it can lead us into grossly immoral actions. The one true loyalty to seek is to morality and righteous living.

Could it be stated that the Nazis had integrity because they had continuity between their words and deeds? Their hateful, evil deeds matched their racist words and beliefs, but they were not virtuous. As the word *loyalty* presupposes an ethical blindness, the word *integrity* presupposes an ethical foundation. For a man to have a fully blossomed integrity, he must be decidedly devoted to morality and moral living. But the man must be careful to live in such a way as his teachings dictate.

Jesus criticized the Pharisees for being inconsistent because what they preached—their ethics—did not match their deeds. They had the opposite of integrity, and Jesus called them hypocrites. We all have standards for how to live. When our actions do not measure up to our standards, there is a gap and we are in jeopardy of being hypocrites.

Integrity, like love, is one of the all-encompassing virtues because it wraps together so many of the other virtues. For instance, as a soldier, I had to learn and constantly repeat the following seven army values: Loyalty, Duty, Respect, Selfless Service, Honor, Integrity, and Personal Courage. Yet, when I studied them, I found that there is truly only one virtue in the list. All of the others are either words or deeds, and for them to achieve what the army wants them to achieve, they must be anchored in morality. But morality is not one of the values, so this value system seems detached from a moral code unless one rightly infers that integrity holds the moral compass for all of the other values.

Integrity not only encompasses many good words and many good deeds; it means that a man's words are followed up by his deeds. That he is not duplicitous, a poser. That what he says, he enacts. Therefore, words plus deeds make up integrity, and also deeds equaling words create integrity. In one case it is a sum; in the other case, a ratio.

*　*　*　*

The reason an entire chapter is devoted to defining the word *integrity*—when others might complete the task in one sentence—is that our culture has evolved away from a common understanding of a moral code. Society has ever-so-dangerously replaced a traditional moral code (a.k.a. the Ten Commandments and the Beatitudes) with a personal code—that whatever you believe in your heart to be your moral compass is true and good for you. Not only has our culture personalized morality—people have made it situational, which means a person does not have to be consistent. If I believe a character trait to be moral one week and I switch my views the next week, there is no inconsistency, because the modern moral compass is based on each situation. This philosophy is all sail and no anchor. Call it relativism or pragmatism, it is a worldview that can lead to a lot of damaged relationships.

In a *National Review* article,[2] Jonah Goldberg speaks about societal shifting on the definition of integrity.

> There was a time when this desire to do good in all things was considered the *only* kind of integrity. . . . But something in the culture has changed. Through virtually the entire history of Western civilization, heroes . . . did good out of a desire to do good— and that good was directed by some external ideal. Sure, it wasn't always, strictly speaking, a Biblical definition of good. . . . But however "good" was defined, it existed in some sort of Platonic realm outside of the protagonist's own id. . . .The hero clung to a definition of "good" that was outside himself, and therefore something he had to reach for.
>
> Not anymore. Now everyone reaches inward for his own vision of integrity. Or, as Omar Little says in *The Wire*, "A man got to have a code."[3]

There are not many paragraphs in this book arguing the basis for a universal moral code. It is assumed. I appreciate the words of C. S. Lewis on the subject in his book *Mere*

Christianity. When confronted with the question of whether morality is subjective or objective, he argues for the latter, stating there is fundamental agreement throughout history and across cultures that an objective morality as found in the Bible exists today. He writes,

I need only ask the reader to think what a totally different morality would mean. Think of a country where people were admired for running away in battle, or where a man felt proud of doublecrossing all the people who had been kindest to him. You might just as well try to imagine a country where two and two made five. Men have differed as regards what people you ought to be unselfish to—whether it was only your own family, or your fellow countrymen, or everyone. But they have always agreed that you ought not to put yourself first. Selfishness has never been admired. Men have differed as to whether you should have one wife or four. But they have always agreed that you must not simply have any woman you liked.[4]

For Christians, our moral code originates from Scripture. We know to be kind, gentle, and patient with others because the Bible has tutored us in these things. *My integrity is how closely my life resembles the teachings that I adhere to.* It is no simpler than that. The Bible is my plumb line for what to say and how to act. Not only does the Bible tell me what to do and what not to do, it tells me that I need integrity to guide my way (Proverbs 11:3); thus, integrity will illuminate the answers to my problems.

The word *integrity* (or *tom* in the Hebrew) is used in the Bible approximately twenty-seven times[5] depending on the translation. It never occurs in the New Testament, and half of its Bible occurrences are in the Psalms and Proverbs. Here is a quick synopsis of what the Bible states about integrity:

- We are to hold fast our integrity in our hearts (Genesis 20:5-6; 1 Kings 9:4; Job 2:3).
- Our integrity is our hope (Job 4:6).
- God will judge us according to our integrity (Job 31:6, Psalm 7:8).
- We are to walk in integrity (Psalm 26:1, 11; 101:2; Proverbs 2:7; 10:9; 19:1; 20:7; 28:6; 28:18).
- We will be upheld by God because of our integrity (Psalm 41:12).
- Our integrity is our guide (Proverbs 11:3).

Now is the time for us to get real. *Are you a man of integrity? Do you desire to be a man of integrity? How do your words and deeds line up?* To have integrity means to live morally upright, to practice what is preached, to walk the talk, and to live the life. It means not having a gap. The man you are in private is the man you are in public. The man you portray at church is the man you are when alone on an out-of-town business trip. It is not easy. It takes guts to live a life of integrity. Living with integrity does not mean being perfect, but it does mean being genuine and consistent.

The Story of Two Roofers

This past spring there was a terrific hailstorm in my hometown. Many homeowners needed to have their roofs replaced; golf-ball-sized hail made indentations in the shingles down into the tar. Like all of my neighbors, I spoke to my insurance company and then petitioned for a roofing company to come validate the damage and provide an estimate for the work.

The first company I called was based on the recommendation of a friend. My friend had not used the roofing company before, but the owner lived in the area and could get to our house quickly. I called and left a message. I called again. Finally, the roofer's wife called me back and we set up an appointment for the inspection. I arranged my schedule to take the day off so I could meet with him. The roofer did not show. I called them back, and his wife said he got busy and could not make it to my house that afternoon, so we set up another appointment. She called again and changed the appointment to later. When the roofer finally showed up, he came to the door and exclaimed he did not bring a ladder and would have to come back another day. I waited a week before I called the company again. His wife said he would try to get back out. That was the last I ever heard from them.

I called a second roofing company and spoke to the owner directly. He told me he would show up that Friday afternoon and perform a thorough inspection. When Friday arrived, the roofer showed up right on time. He took out his ladder, walked the roof, made chalk marks about the hail, and took nearly eighty photos. He stepped into my house afterward and downloaded the photos onto my laptop so I could easily provide them to my insurance company. He explained to me the damage he had seen on the roof—large hits in the vent covers and deeply gouged shingles that indeed needed to be replaced. He was extremely professional and friendly, and he proudly wore his company shirt.

The second roofer is not only someone with whom I want to do business but also the type of man I strive to be: someone trustworthy, whose word means something. The second roofer was a man with integrity. What he said he followed up on; his words matched his deeds. My roof was finished in a timely manner and looks great.

The first roofer was a disaster. In fact, I am glad he never showed up, because I cannot imagine what it would have been like to have a project performed by his company.

When you give someone your word on something, you are giving them a small representation of your life. In older days, men used to spit on their hands before they would shake, representing that a part of their life—their spit—was tied to the promise. When young boys look like their father, they are said to be the spitting image of him, meaning his life (spit) and his reflection (image). Our promises, contracts, and words to other people are in essence our names, our lives, and our reputations extending to them. Being people of integrity is making sure that everything we say is backed by what we do, that we are not living duplicitous lives as posers. Our words matter. Our deeds matter. Our integrity matters. The psalmist tells us that those who keep their word—even when it costs them—may abide in God's home.

> O LORD, who may abide in Your tent?
> Who may dwell on Your holy hill?
> He who walks with integrity, and works righteousness,
> And speaks truth in his heart. . . .
> He swears to his own hurt and does not change.
>
> PSALM 15:1-4

General Douglas MacArthur—whose story started this chapter—was asked by President Roosevelt to change his speech from "I shall return!" to "We shall return!" But MacArthur did not like the suggestion and refused to do so. He felt that the change could open the door to some weaseling in Washington, and he did not want to unnecessarily delay the rescue of millions of Filipino citizens and thousands of American POWs. He kept his speech intact. He kept his word and, further, went on to oversee the surrender of Japan and the end of World War II. A true statesman. Here is a quote from MacArthur:

> If the historian of the future should deem my
> service worthy of some slight reference, it would be
> my hope that he mention me not as a commander
> engaged in campaigns and battles, even though

victorious to American arms, but rather as that one
whose sacred duty it became, once the guns were
silenced, to carry to the land of our vanquished foe
the solace and hope and faith of Christian morals.[6]

CHAPTER 3

AN HONEST ASSESSMENT OF SELF

They are the so-called "impossible" men.

IN 1916, when England was already engulfed in World War I, the US Navy—suspecting things could soon become worse—decided to assemble a group of volunteers who expressed interest in joining the naval services. They endeavored to provide a series of lectures for the volunteers on sea operations, coastal defenses, torpedoes, and military character. For the lecture on character, the organizers asked Captain William Sims to speak to the volunteers. Sims was a good choice because he would soon become the admiral in command of all US naval forces operating in Europe.

"A central but often overlooked element," Captain Sims believed, "was the importance of self-awareness. Professionalism requires a constant personal net assessment, or 'estimate of the situation.'"[1] The future military leaders listened attentively to their speaker. "It seems almost incredible that there should be men of marked intellectual capacity, extensive professional knowledge and experience, energy and professional enthusiasm, who have been a detriment to the service in every position they have occupied," Sims lectured. "They are the so-called 'impossible' men who have left throughout their careers a trail of discontent and insubordination; all because of their ignorance of, or neglect of, one or many of the essential attributes of military character."

Just as Captain Sims strongly encouraged men to be self-aware of their character in his speech given one hundred years ago, this chapter will allow you to take an honest self-assessment of your words and deeds. The beginning of this chapter contains a forty-question inventory, which will place you into one of four categories. The more honestly you answer each question, the more effectively this book will increase your self-awareness. Please know that the point of this quick assessment is not for you to try to have a perfect score, because everyone will be different. It is to show you where you are at *now*, and to give you a starting point for life change.

I recently asked a man if he wanted to take the diagnostic, and he told me he would not do so until he knew exactly what answers I was trying to get out of him. I told him it was not an exam but a tool to reflect where he currently was in his life with words and deeds. Only honest answering, a snapshot of where he was right now, would help him.

He was not satisfied with this explanation and declared that he would only take the diagnostic if he could research each question to discover how to get a perfect score. He missed the point entirely. The diagnostic is not an exam; it is a mirror: The more honestly you respond to the questions, the sharper the image you will have of yourself.

One of the greatest literary works in history is a book called *The Brothers Karamazov.* Hear how Fyodor Dostoyevsky describes honesty in self-assessment.

> Above all, don't lie to yourself. The man who lies to himself and listens to his own lie comes to such a pass that he cannot distinguish the truth within him, or around him, and so loses all respect for himself and for others. And having no respect he ceases to love.[2]

The Words and Deeds Diagnostic

In 2015, I found myself wondering if there was a way for men to know the state of their character when it came to words and deeds. The process began by leading a Bible study for military members at Fort Bragg, North Carolina. The study was accompanied by a simple graph whereby men could chart their words and their deeds. Months of revising, working with hundreds of men, and asking lots of questions produced the following assessment tool, which has been field-tested by men from a variety of backgrounds, including those who work in the trades, young men from universities and service academies, those retired, those who own their own businesses, and pastors who serve in the ministry full-time. The following diagnostic was vetted by helpful leaders at the Army Research Institute for the Behavioral and Social Sciences at Fort Belvoir, Virginia, and it has yielded tremendous results for individuals searching for feedback on where they stand in the continuity spectrum of their words and deeds. It is considered a multisource (or 360 degree) device because it also allows men to receive feedback from other people who know them intimately.

DIRECTIONS: Please check either "a" or "b" for each question, marking the answer that sounds the most like you. When you have completed the diagnostic, there will be a simple scoring method.

1. When I hear something that does not sound quite accurate, I . . .

_____ a. Immediately correct the person speaking

_____ b. Look for an opportunity to approach the matter diplomatically

2. In an honest assessment of how I come through for people, I . . .

_____ a. Sometimes overpromise and underdeliver

_____ b. Always do more than what's expected

3. I am more likely to . . .

_____ a. Avoid controversial subjects

_____ b. Say what's on my mind

4. My friends would say they . . .

_____ a. Sometimes can't rely on me

_____ b. Count on me to do the right thing

5. In stressful situations I usually . . .

_____ a. Tell people the cold, hard truth

_____ b. Say words to make others feel better

6. I am the kind of person who is . . .

_____ a. Often called genuine or authentic

_____ b. Sometimes called a prankster or a button pusher

7. At work it is more natural for me to . . .

_____ a. Point out how others can improve

_____ b. Encourage others

8. I have a knack for knowing what to do.

_____ a. Nearly all of the time

_____ b. Sometimes

9. When meeting new people, I . . .

_____ a. Love to ask them questions to find out who
they are

_____ b. Like to listen and observe to see what kind
of person they are

10. I am more drawn to . . .

_____ a. Letting things happen naturally

_____ b. Working hard and playing hard

11. When I am on a team, I am the spokesman.

_____ a. Occasionally, but not usually

_____ b. Nearly always

12. An observer would notice that when I am on a team,
I usually . . .

_____ a. Seek for a job that will match my skills

_____ b. Volunteer for the job no one wants

13. When I make a commitment that's turning
sour, I . . .

_____ a. Stick to it, even at personal cost

_____ b. Rationalize why another course might
be better

14. In getting to work, I tend to . . .

_____ a. Arrive early, so I am prepared for the day

_____ b. Cut it close, and occasionally arrive late

15. When meeting a deadline and trying to get things done, I can be . . .

_____ a. Sometimes short with others, hoping they will understand

_____ b. Just as polite as when I'm relaxed

16. When making important decisions, I usually . . .

_____ a. Forge ahead to see what doors will open

_____ b. Look at everything thoroughly to avoid risks

17. When people around me are critical of others, I sometimes . . .

_____ a. Stick up for those not present, even though it creates tension

_____ b. Remain silent and regret it later

18. I tend to . . .

_____ a. Pick and choose at some length as to what to be involved in

_____ b. Overcommit myself to important projects

19. As far as honesty is concerned . . .

_____ a. I sometimes exaggerate to make the story better

_____ b. Others never have to worry about the truth of my stories

20. My friends would say that I am great at following up on things.

_____ a. It depends on who you ask

_____ b. All of them would say that

21. My friends . . .

_____ a. Always count on me to say the right thing

_____ b. Are sometimes surprised at what comes out of my mouth

22. I am known as a person who likes tackling tough jobs.

_____ a. That is an accurate statement

_____ b. Not everyone sees me that way

23. If I haven't heard from someone in a while, we finally connect when . . .

_____ a. They reach out and connect with me

_____ b. I reach out and connect with them

24. When under stress at work, I usually . . .

_____ a. Am forceful with coworkers without attacking them personally

_____ b. Am calm toward my coworkers but sometimes redirect the angst to others

25. When telling a story, I . . .

_____ a. Love to explain all the details so people understand

_____ b. Keep it short so I don't bore anyone

26. When volunteers are needed, I . . .

_____ a. Usually wait for others to take the lead

_____ b. Often raise my hand first

27. When trying to convince someone of something complex, I . . .

_____ a. Get right to the point, with as few details as possible

_____ b. Take the necessary time and approach it from several different angles

28. I am known for being sluggish sometimes.

_____ a. True

_____ b. False

29. I am known as a person with great empathy.

_____ a. True

_____ b. False

30. During a project, an observer might notice that I . . .

_____ a. Work hard until the job is 100 percent
finished

_____ b. Sometimes take a break when the job is
90 percent finished

31. I do not hesitate to ask for clarification from my boss
or coworkers.

_____ a. No, I prefer to figure things out on my own

_____ b. As needed

32. I sometimes don't respond right away when others
reach out to me.

_____ a. No, this doesn't describe me

_____ b. Occasionally

33. I listen well when others are telling a story.

_____ a. All the time

_____ b. Some of the time

34. My friends would say I am a person with . . .

_____ a. Great ideas

_____ b. Great accomplishments

35. My friends would say that I am a great conversationalist.

_____ a. It depends on who you ask

_____ b. All of them would say that

36. When playing games or solving problems, I . . .

_____ a. Stick with tried-and-true methods of success

_____ b. Look for unorthodox ways to succeed

37. In conversations, I sometimes compliment people to gain their trust.

_____ a. True

_____ b. False

38. I help others with how to improve their lives.

_____ a. Continually

_____ b. Sometimes

39. I try to influence others by . . .

_____ a. Hoping they will learn from my behavior

_____ b. Making them laugh until they warm up to me

40. With home improvement projects, my family would say that I . . .

_____ a. Seek projects to complete in my free time

_____ b. Take care of something only when it is urgent

*   *   *   *

Diagnostic Scoring Sheet

Please write your answers ("a" or "b") next to the numbers below:

COLUMN I	COLUMN II	COLUMN III	COLUMN IV	COLUMN V	COLUMN VI	COLUMN VII	COLUMN VIII
1.	2.	3.	4.	5.	6.	7.	8.
9.	10.	11.	12.	13.	14.	15.	16.
17.	18.	19.	20.	21.	22.	23.	24.
25.	26.	27.	28.	29.	30.	31.	32.
33.	34.	35.	36.	37.	38.	39.	40.
SUM							

INSTRUCTIONS: For columns I, V, VI, and VIII, add the "a" responses and write the sum on the line in the row entitled "Sum." For columns II, III, IV, and VII, add the "b" responses and write the sum in the space provided.

Results from Odd Columns → Column I Sum: _____ + Column III Sum: _____ + Column V Sum: _____ + Column VII Sum: _____ = _____ Total # of WORDS

Results from Even Columns → Column II Sum: _____ + Column IV Sum: _____ + Column VI Sum: _____ + Column VIII Sum: _____ = _____ Total # of DEEDS

My results: _____ Words _____ Deeds

- 0–10 Words with 0–10 Deeds = Sentry
- 11–20 Words with 0–10 Deeds = Salesman
- 0–10 Words with 11–20 Deeds = Scout
- 11–20 Words with 11–20 Deeds = Statesman

This means that I am a _____.

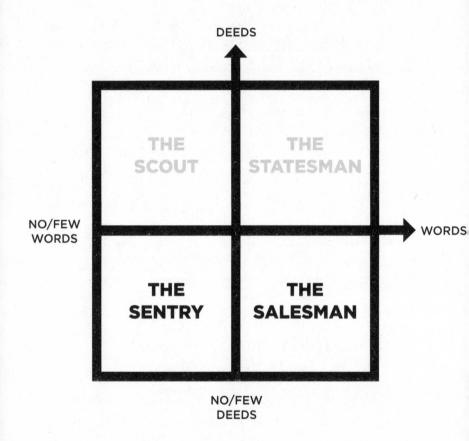

CHAPTER 4

THE SENTRY AND THE SALESMAN

For I knew that you were a hard man.

"WHAT KIND OF MAN ARE YOU?" It is a question that probably has entered the mind of every man alive. It is difficult to answer: Is there only one kind of man? Are there as many "kinds" of men as there are men? As pertains to character, I'd like to suggest, there are only four. The assessment you took in the previous chapter yields insight into which of the four describes you today. The good news is that these four types are descriptors, not predictors: If you're not the kind of man you want to be today, there's work you can do to become that man in the future.

This chapter and the next one explain the differences between each character type and clarify how each type tends to respond to four important areas of life:

- (R) Relationships;
- (S) Stress;
- (T) Teamwork; and
- (L) Leadership opportunities.

The following four profiles are snapshots, fluid categories that can change over time and are only a small part of the uniqueness of each person. To test as one type does not mean everything one does falls into the pattern of that type. Some men close to another type will have tendencies that are not the norm for their test-result type. Also, men who choose to work on the tools provided in the later chapters of this book will gradually move to another type and will not be forever anchored into the quadrant they initially received. Please remember, the following profiles will hopefully prove to be very helpful, but they represent a current snapshot, based on how the questions were answered today, and they should never be used in an effort to understand the totality of a person. They are simply a runner's starting block, placed intentionally on the track to use as an impetus for forward progress.

The Sentry (Words: ↓; Deeds: ↓)

The type of man I call "the Sentry" is so named because, in the truest sense of the word, a sentry stands guard, immobile, with no words, quietly guarding his post. A sentry will not leave his post until he is properly relieved. There are no words and no actions, except to guard the position assigned to him. Many men in our society function as Sentries, men who quietly guard something, something of value, perhaps only to them. It might be their peace of mind. They wait to be relieved, but it never happens, because they have neither asked for it nor worked for it. They are not overly wordy or encouragers, and they are not proactive nor do they typically hold many important accomplishments. Sentries are satisfied with the motto that life is easier if you just let it ride. They are the men outside the arena.

We all have someone in our lives who is a Sentry. These are the guys who are not making any waves. You see them at church or work and they are cordial, but you never have the sense that they truly care about you or the current interaction. It is almost as if they cannot wait to get out of the building and go home to where they feel more comfortable. But do not be mistaken; the Sentry's life is somewhat uncomfortable at home as well. He simply goes through the motions in life: getting married, raising kids, being a steady churchman or a good employee.

Some Sentry men are oblivious to the fact that there is a lot more to life that they can grab and hold on to. The unaware Sentry is the most pitiable type. The Sentry may not feel as if he is struggling with life, but he is certainly causing others to struggle. Not very stellar with his words or his deeds, the Sentry is more the quiet type and the inactive type.

Please recall the four important components of life mentioned in this chapter's introduction: Relationships (R), times of Stress (S), Teamwork (T), and opportunities in Leadership (L). Each character type will be rated between one and four stars for the four components. A one- or two-star rating means improvement is recommended. Here is a look at how the Sentry typically responds in the R, S, T, and L areas of life:

(★) **Relationships**—The Sentry may struggle with his most important relationships. Those closest to the Sentry see his potential and wish the Sentry would reach out to grab the future and improve himself. When this repeatedly does not happen, disappointment can turn to bitterness. The Sentry lets others down, can be unreliable, and fails to communicate properly with others when the time calls for it. Of all four types, the Sentry causes the largest disappointments in this crucial area of life. He sometimes operates like he is the only one impacted by his lack of words and deeds and tends to carry an "every man for himself" attitude.

(★) **Stress**—The Sentry does not do well under stress. He often acts like stress does not bother him, but deep down he can be in a panic. He tends to bury issues that truly bother him. However, when the Sentry stresses out, there is probably a good reason for his worry. Without building relationships with gracious words and achieving positive accomplishments with deeds, these under-performers can spiral downward in a hurry. Life is not against a Sentry, but he can feel this way. When not surrounded by trusting relationships, the Sentry can assume others do not care about him or are out to get him. "Why are you trying to ruin my life?" he might think, when the other party is simply trying to assist. Of all the types, the Sentry worries about the future the most, yet—ironically—does little to implement life change.

(★) **Teamwork**—The Sentry will struggle with teamwork. Usually, he becomes the team spoiler, discrediting the importance of the mission or of those leading it. When either confronted or ignored, he might totally disengage. The Sentry may think that all of his thoughts and ideas are the right ones, and others simply do not understand the true state of things. However, as other people advance ideas or initiate new actions, the Sentry can remain quiet and inactive. When forced to participate, the Sentry might bring up something that worked previously for him, even though it may not fit the present context. In this situation, blinding pride prevents true discussion and engagement.

(★) **Leadership**—The passive Sentry should not occupy a position of leadership. When a Sentry leads, communication does not reach subordinates, goals are not accomplished, and the organization suffers. Sometimes he runs over others because he sees what the organization needs but has no idea how to get there. Employees supervised by a Sentry sense he is only in it for himself or that he blindly follows the rules, even to the detriment of his coworkers. Further, a Sentry underestimates how challenging it is to lead and sometimes scoffs at the leaders around him. He does not comprehend the maxim that the best leaders are good followers. If the Sentry were to look at his own life objectively, he would see that although he has some gifts, he is not using them. It is like the parable of the servant who buried the one talent his master entrusted to him for an investment because he knew that his master was a hard man. It did not go well for him when his master returned and wanted an accounting (Matthew 25:24-30). God gives men gifts so they can serve others and live productive lives, not so they can squander life. Nothing drives parents more crazy than when they have a smart child who simply forgets to turn in his homework or never does it out of laziness. The Sentry can aggravate those around him—especially a visionary, who sees potential in everyone around him—because others know that he can do better.

The good news is that the Sentry's life is fairly black and white, so life change is more obvious, pressing, and easily attained. Members of the other three types already have a certain amount of successes, which may blind them to needing a corrective. The Sentry does not have success to hinder his forward progress. He might sense he needs to change because people around him have been either asking him to change or quietly praying for him to change. Of all four types, the Sentry has the most potential.

Some Sentries acknowledge things are not quite right. Though all four types of men can perceive a disconnect between the men they want to be and the men they truly are, it can be the most painful for the Sentry because this is a larger chasm for him than it is for the other types. I call this *the gap*, and it is explained in detail in chapter 7. The gap is agonizing and possesses an eternal, dull ache. For some, it might feel like an everlasting desire that is perennially unattainable. For other men in the Sentry category, those bound by addictions or pain so acute it immobilizes them, the passions in life are deeply and secretly sapped with time.

In conclusion, there are many good men who are Sentries. They hold steady jobs, live quiet lives, and stay committed to their families. However, there is something slightly apathetic with a Sentry. He does not live his life with purpose. The Sentry might know how to alter himself, and might have even gone to a life-success conference or read a book on life change, but he simply has not found the discipline to stick to it and experience true life transformation. Those Sentries who scored close to another type may feel things acutely or be deeply affected by issues in their relationships, but they tend to hide their vulnerability behind a veneer of detachment. Perhaps more than any other type, the Sentry has the propensity to hold on to either the past or a wish-dream of how life should work, which ultimately can hinder his ability to make decisions or find joy in life.

The following statements will likely grab the Sentry's attention:

- Take all the time you need.
- What's all the fuss about?
- I'm doing the best I can.
- It's not the end of the world.
- Live and let live.

THE
SENTRY

POSITIVES

+ Takes life as it comes

+ Not worried about appearances

+ Satisfied with simplicity

NEGATIVES

- Every man for himself (R)

- Buries issues; others out to get him (S)

- Team irritant (T)

- Passive; too apathetic to create lasting change (L)

Quick Takeaways for the Sentry Type:

1. Passivity
2. Loads of potential
3. Would not tolerate following a leader like himself
4. Few encouraging words for others
5. Easygoing attitude, but potentially a cover-up for the storm inside

The Salesman (Words: ↑; Deeds: ↓)

Imagine you attend church one Sunday with your kids and you meet a nice family man. The father introduces himself, tells you where he works, and says how long he has attended that church. He might tell you what position he holds in his corporation or mention a promotion he recently received. Then, he seeks to solicit information from you in the conversation. However, after spending a moment with this individual, you might discover that he is asking you questions only so he can talk more about himself and his family. You might also notice that he does not really hear you when you are talking but is thinking of the next thing he is going to say. He could even interrupt you to get in his own words.

Everyone has a male friend who talks a lot. They're great at parties because you never have to worry about a lull. They're great at brainstorming because they never stop storming (although sometimes their brains may seem to check out). They occasionally wear you out, and sometimes you notice that their big ideas rarely touch the ground, their strong opinions are seldom rooted in experience, and their jokes aren't tempered by consideration for the needs of others. They're words people—that much is clear. But deeds? Those are harder to see in their lives. I call this type of man "the Salesman."

Everyone exercises influence in some way, but men who fall into the Salesman category primarily influence people with their words. An important reminder for this study is that in and of themselves, words are not bad. Words are helpful. But they are much more impactful when in proportion to concurrent deeds. Imbalanced words and deeds force one to struggle with the four important life components mentioned in this chapter's introduction: Relationships (R), times of Stress (S), Teamwork (T), and opportunities in Leadership (L). Importantly, note that the Salesman possesses one of two types: He could either be a great communicator who truly cares about others or a prideful man who is more focused on himself and how others view him. Here is a look at how the Salesman typically responds in the R, S, T, and L areas of life:

(★★★) **Relationships**—The Salesman is often the life of the party. He is easy to get along with and functions well when a relationship needs work because he is able to talk things out. Sometimes, however, people communicating with the Salesman become annoyed with his slightly disingenuous ways. The Salesman might seem like a best friend one day but then appear shallow by moving on to other people exceedingly fast. Overall, though, relationships are a strength for the Salesman.

(★★) **Stress**—Under stress, the Salesman may not be very well equipped. His deeds have not matched his words. It is similar to the man who built his house on the sand. The externals are fine, but there is not a strong foundation. Sometimes life comes crashing down in a hurry when there is a storm. The Salesman can make seemingly erratic or impulsive decisions, which could harm him or his loved ones.

(★★★) **Teamwork**—The Salesman works well in a team environment. He is usually the team spokesman—not necessarily out of selfless service, but often because he simply wants a platform to talk. He can annoy the team leader, because the Salesman sometimes publicly generates alternative ideas on how the leader should lead. A Salesman can also stifle other team members who are more hesitant to speak up, like the Scout or Sentry. However, Teamwork is considered a strength, because the Salesman knows how to connect with people.

(★★) **Leadership**—This is a mixed bag. Depending on his personality type, a Salesman can be a good leader or a bad leader. A humble Salesman spends his time encouraging those around him, hoping all in the organization benefit from a job well done. With other Salesmen, however, it can be "my way or the highway," and they do not allow room for alternative opinions. The reason Leadership is only two stars is because those who like to work independently can often feel smothered by the wordy Salesman who continually interrupts his subordinates. What's worse, he will then take credit for the work, often without knowing all the details of the project.

I call this type a Salesman not because to work in sales is to elevate words and neglect deeds. In fact, an important quality of a good salesman is the ability to listen to his customers and adequately respond to their needs and desires. But a salesman is, almost iconically, a conversationalist. A good salesman can sell anything, from cars to computers to clothes to cakes, because he concentrates his efforts on the conversation that leads to the sale. A good salesman doesn't have to be able to rebuild an engine or read and write programming code; a good salesman has to guide a good conversation.

However, without a proportionate amount of deeds, a Salesman (for this study) could be a man who agrees in conversation to help you with projects but then does not show up; or the man who repeatedly says that you should get together but then never responds to your e-mail or text; or the man who continually threatens to give management a piece of his mind, though you know he will never follow through. Everyone has met other men like this. This is the classic Salesman, who is high on words and low on deeds. Perhaps you have experienced a classroom setting where the leader asks if anyone has questions and then a hand goes up. But the Salesman's question isn't really a question; it is a statement of facts to portray to everyone in the class—especially the leader—that the question asker is present, attentive, and smart.

In a positive way, some Salesmen use their ease with words to build relationships and network with others. They can do a lot of good to help make society function, but without a proportionate amount of good deeds, the Salesman builds up himself, not others. Jesus said to allow others to see your good deeds so that they, too, can glorify the Father in heaven (Matthew 5:16). With more words than deeds, we promote self.

Plentiful words are not the issue here; the world needs both introverts and extroverts to function. People often assume that Salesmen are extroverts, but an introvert can just as easily be a Salesman type. The issue is not the quantity of words people use—everyone talks, some more than others—but the extent to which a person is known for speaking in contrast to doing. A windbag who is "all talk and no action" (throws around a lot of ideas but rarely executes those ideas), "all bark and no bite" (talks boldly behind someone's back but never confronts them directly), or "all hat and no cattle" (identifies himself with an activity or accomplishment that isn't reflected in his life history)—whether introverted or extroverted, such a person is, as Shakespeare lamented in *Macbeth*,

> *A poor player*
> *That struts and frets his hour upon the stage . . .*
> *Full of sound and fury,*
> *Signifying nothing.*[1]

When the words of a man are predominant over his actions, it leaves something to be desired. Sometimes the Salesman is everyone's friend, but he may not hold a deep relationship with anyone.

The following statements will likely grab the Salesman's attention:

- What do you think of this?
- What is the plan?
- How are you feeling?

THE SALESMAN

POSITIVES

+ Outgoing and friendly (R)

+ Makes deals

+ Team spokesman (T)

+ Life of the party

+ Makes others feel at ease

NEGATIVES

- Erratic and impulsive (S)

- Can be a wolf in sheepskin

- My way or the highway (L)

- Deals are self-focused

- Perceived shallowness

- We're having a reunion.
- There are some people I'd like you to meet.

Quick Takeaways for the Salesman Type:
1. Promises made by the Salesman are not necessarily inviolable contracts
2. Communicates well with others
3. May not always sound genuine
4. Many words and many friends

This chapter looked at the first two kinds of men as it pertains to character. Please remember that these types are descriptors, not predictors: If you're not the kind of man you want to be today, there's work you can do to become that man in the future. The next chapter deals with the other two types of men: those with high deeds and low words, and those with high words and high deeds.

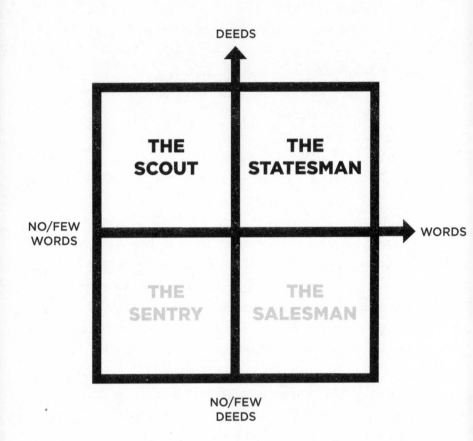

CHAPTER 5

THE SCOUT AND THE STATESMAN

They had that special grace, that special spirit that says,
"Give me a challenge, and I'll meet it with joy."

THE FOLLOWING CHAPTER IS FOR MEN who assessed into either the Scout (low words, high deeds) or the Statesman (high words and deeds) categories. As mentioned previously, these profiles are snapshots, fluid categories that can change over time and are only a small part of the uniqueness of each person. To test as one type does not mean everything one does falls into the pattern of that type.

The Scout (Words: ↓; Deeds: ↑)

Imagine you are at work and your supervisor asks you to work on a project with a coworker that you do not know very well. When you get to know this individual, you find out many interesting things about him. For instance, while working on the project together, you notice how quiet he is as he goes about his work. Quiet is nice, but sometimes you're looking for a little connection with the people you work closely with, so you try initiating conversation. "This project sure is interesting," you say. "Someday, I wouldn't mind starting a little cottage industry doing something like this."

"You should," your coworker replies. "I started a nonprofit last year. It's a lot of work, but it's fun." He goes quiet, but a few strategic questions draw him out and you hear a fascinating tale of entrepreneurship. The next week you ask him what he's doing over the weekend. "I'm running an Ironman down by the lake," he replies. An Ironman?!? You had no idea! A few more probing questions and you've heard another fascinating story. Each week is the same— quiet work punctuated by incredible stories only prompted by your questions. He's not bragging, he's simply answering. You have just met a Scout. He did not tell you those things prematurely; they came out in the natural course of your conversation as you asked questions about his life. If those actions belonged to a Salesman, he would have already mentioned it or recruited you to participate in his activities.

The type of man I call "the Scout" has a life more focused on accomplishments than words; often when you meet one, you appreciate him. An actual scout is a soldier or spy sent ahead of the main force to gather information about the enemy's position, strength, or movements. An essential ingredient for a scout is that he is stealthy and—unlike the Salesman—does not attract a lot of attention. He performs deeds and reports back, and when executing a mission, he is expected to be quiet. Here is a look at how the Scout typically responds in the R, S, T, and L areas of life:

(★★) **Relationships**—The Scout can be frustrated with relationships because he underestimates the importance of words. He might also suffer by not communicating the care and concern that he feels in his heart for someone he loves. His wife and children need the Scout to speak words of truth into their lives and to do it genuinely, not just on Valentine's Day, when he thinks it is required. The Scout has a lot in his heart and mind; he just struggles to get his words out in a meaningful way to positively impact others.

(★★★) **Stress**—The Scout handles stress much better than the Salesman. Because Scouts have more deeds than words, they are usually more prepared for unfortunate circumstances. For instance, a Scout may be quietly saving money for a rainy day, and in an area vulnerable to natural disaster, a Scout has an emergency kit ready and close at hand. The downside is that although a Scout may appear more calm, he could be brewing a storm on the inside and be in a lot of pain. A Salesman will blow up onto those around him; a Scout will blow up inside.

(★★★) **Teamwork**—This is another positive aspect for the Scout. Usually a solid team builder, the Scout contributes to the team by listening to the leader and doing things behind the scenes for his boss. Sometimes, if the Scout decides to play it safe and not engage with others, he can bring down a team, but usually he is a solid workhorse who executes the mission. A downside here is that with a lack of communication, the Scout may set off in a direction not necessarily best for the team. However, a good leader can rein him in easily.

(★★) **Leadership**—The Scout can struggle with leadership, although he is placed in a position to lead others frequently. A Scout is more quiet and presumed competent at first. Then, he struggles to effectively engage those around him. Sometimes the Scout is not very verbal with those in his organization. Nothing drives subordinates more crazy than receiving a bad annual evaluation for an issue never brought to their attention by their supervisor during the work year. A Scout struggles with being direct and speaking the plain, hard truth. He often avoids confrontations and does not allow his words to build bridges into the hearts and minds of those around him. The good news is that when a Scout perceives this struggle, he can quickly turn it around, because the deeds are already in place.

Even a fool, when he keeps silent, is considered wise;
When he closes his lips, he is considered prudent.

PROVERBS 17:28

People are often pleasantly surprised by a Scout because there is more to him than meets the eye. Scouts are men whose deeds outshine their words, which are few. Sometimes, they are referred to as the "silent type," but it is not mere introversion that defines a Scout; that would be too simplistic an analysis. The Scout might be very comfortable in social settings and be energized by being with people. What sets him apart is that he is a man of action, of accomplishments, and—sometimes—of great skills. Scouts do not flaunt their deeds; often, they allow the deeds to speak for themselves.

The downside for Scouts is that they do not allow their words to build bridges into others' lives. They are not necessarily self-focused, but their great deeds are not aligned with their words. They may have no words. A lack of words is sometimes harmful in relationships, corporations, or the military. Imagine having a commander who expects you to know what he is thinking or assumes you know the 5 W's (who, what, when, where, and why) of the next mission. The Scout's deeds might be good, but without the right mix of words and deeds, the Scout could remain ineffective in life. The nonprofit may never get off the ground if the Scout has not mentioned it to anyone. As a coach, the Scout may not communicate his plans to win the game, so his team might be

THE SCOUT

POSITIVES

+ Coolness/calmness

+ Maintains composure (S)

+ Team builder (T)

+ Quiet loyalist

+ Behind-the-scenes worker

NEGATIVES

- Can miss opportunities

- May be perceived as non-engaging (R)

- Unable to communicate deep feelings

- Expects people to read his mind (L)

confused about their strategy. Subordinates might get a different rating from their Scout supervisor than they expected.

Unlike the Salesman, who displays more words than deeds, the Scout prefers deeds more than words, but when deeds are complemented by a proportionate amount of words, much more can be accomplished in life. The Salesman thrives when he makes a connection with someone and likes when people "get" him. The Scout thrives when he is *doing* something for someone and likes when people leave him alone.

Finally, similar to the Salesman, there are two types of Scouts. One type of Scout uses his deeds to promote good for others and does not care for any recognition. He simply does not engage well with others verbally, so he is limited in that respect. The other type of Scout does his deeds mostly for personal glory and praise. He works hard to gain medals, but it all circles back to nothingness because of his desire to promote self, which ends in vanity.

The following statements will likely grab the Scout's attention:

- You can make a difference here.
- Can you help me?
- Can you speak privately with me about something?
- We've got a complex problem that needs a solution.
- This is a secret mission where stealth is required.
- Let's cut to the chase.

Quick Takeaways for the Scout Type:
1. Source of effectiveness is accomplishments
2. Usually surprises others with his depth
3. Loves other people but can struggle communicating affection
4. Behind-the-scenes worker

The Statesman (Words: ↑; Deeds: ↑)

The final type of man is the Statesman. His words and deeds are aligned, making him a man of integrity and influence.

In the strictest sense of the word, a statesman is an envoy or ambassador, someone who negotiates treaties on behalf of nations. Statesmen are leaders of leaders. In this study, the Statesman is a man who uses his words to magnify the effectiveness of his deeds. In the army we would say his words become combat or force multipliers—tools that amplify the effort and produce greater-than-expected output.

Unlike the other types, there are not two bents, or multiple possibilities, for the Statesman; what you see is what you get. There is not one type of Statesman that is selfish and another Statesman that is simply inhibited. The priorities of a Statesman's life are aligned, and he follows through on his commitments. All men struggle with selfishness and self-centeredness, but the Statesman is aware of these self-tendencies and thus intentionally strives to put other people first. He can mentor others and use his life as a model because he makes good decisions and is honest and genuine.

Sometimes we meet Statesmen at work, at church, or on the ball field. They are the men who have a good attitude whether they experience victory or defeat, and they encourage others to do their best. It is refreshing to speak to Statesmen because they ask good questions and are more interested in hearing others speak than in hearing themselves talk.

A Statesman's interest in others is contrasted by his disinterest in gaining any advantage from them. Others can sense his sincerity and know that he is disinclined to leverage the new relationship to his advantage, that the Statesman only wants to be a friend, with no strings attached. This sincerity is what is so refreshing about interacting with this type! Statesmen are primarily focused on other people; they build their lives upon the bedrock of selfless service. Their identity is fully formed, they know who they are, and they accept their position as sinners who receive grace. Here is a look at how the Statesman typically responds in the R, S, T, and L areas of life:

(★★★★) **Relationships**—The Statesman does well in this important area of life. As with the Salesman and Scout, people are very important to the Statesman, and he makes them feel important by showing that he cares about them. The Statesman is quick to listen and loves other people in spite of their issues or failures. Those closest to the Statesman know that he is not perfect, but he is quick to own his mistakes and speedy to forgive others, and he does not hold grudges. The Statesman is loyal in all of his relationships, especially to his family members. He can be counted on when he makes a commitment, and this dependability builds trust in those around him.

(★★★★) **Stress**—The Statesman handles stress well because he knows who is in charge of his destiny. Like the man in the parable who built his house on a rock, the Statesman has made solid life decisions, which gives him strength when times grow hard. It is not that calamity does not come to

him, but that, when it does come, the Statesman
keeps it in perspective: He knows that, in addition
to prayer and perseverance, sometimes the right
response involves words (e.g., what Reagan said
after the *Challenger* explosion[1]) and sometimes it
involves deeds (e.g., how Eisenhower responded
to the Little Rock debacle[2]). As with relationships,
teamwork, and leadership, stress also influences
other people. Because the Statesman navigates
stormy waters without an emotional shipwreck,
people grow to trust him and seek his counsel.
The Statesman gets angry about the right things
but does not let his emotions influence him into
bad decisions.

(★★★★) **Teamwork**—Though teamwork is also
a strength for the Salesman and the Scout, the
Statesman is even better at this category. When
he is part of a team, the Statesman listens to
instructions, asks appropriate questions regarding
the task at hand, spends adequate time identifying
the problem, and works with the team to find a
solution. He is the first to jump in and do the
dirty work. The Statesman is collaborative and
innovative. When the team begins to sway off
course, the Statesman is there as a corrective to steer
the team back onto the right path. The Statesman's
contributions in words and deeds are usually

evident; as a result, team leadership often ultimately falls to him.

(★★★★) **Leadership**—When placed in leadership, the Statesman is active and leads by example. He articulates a clear vision, then he equips subordinates with the tools they need for their tasks. The Statesman embodies the values of the organization he is a part of. He often overachieves, tells subordinates "thank you" to the point of excess, and credits the entire team when successful. The Statesman does not nitpick or micromanage his subordinates because he *wants* them to work independently. He trusts people. The Statesman is not worried about impressing those above him; he simply wants to do a good job. He does not commit to a task because it would look good to others; he commits his team to a task because it is the right thing for his organization to do, even when it makes him unpopular. The Statesman can laugh at himself when he makes a mistake, and he admits it to those around him. He meets with team members regularly, and though he does not hold grudges, he holds people responsible for their work and expects his workers to be good stewards. This is the rare man who will take a hit before he allows harm to come to one of his loyal followers, even at great personal cost. The Statesman is always gracious and giving, and people are loyal to him because they've experienced his integrity and honest behavior. Workers trust a Statesman to treat them right. He builds his team by anchoring all of his relationships in a sea of trust.

Though I have listed each of the above areas with four stars, the Statesman category still has room for improvement. No one is perfect, even those who score "20" for words and "20" for deeds. Remember, the diagnostic device represents a current snapshot, based on how the questions were answered today, and results should never be considerd comprehensive.

THE STATESMAN

POSITIVES

+ Loyal and true (R)

+ Enthusiastic

+ Keeps perspective (S)

+ Has conviction

+ Team leader (T)

+ Has integrity

+ Active, trusts workers, leads by example, and makes good decisions (L)

There is always opportunity for growth, understanding of others, and self-discovery.

The Statesman is called by God and knows that this call trumps the fear of man. He recognizes and utilizes an alternative strength to accomplish his tasks. He inspires other people with his sense of purpose and passion to help his fellow man. The Statesman is humble, knowing that it is only by God's grace that he operates, and he has a larger perspective, knowing that God's plans are always bigger than the players. Even in work environments of pride, greed, and selfishness, the Statesman maintains his sense of humility and selflessness.

For the Statesman, 2 Peter 1:8 comes to mind: "If you possess these qualities [goodness, knowledge, self-control, perseverance, godliness, kindness, and love] in increasing measure, they will keep you from being ineffective and unproductive in your knowledge of our Lord Jesus Christ" (NIV).

The Statesman is led by the Spirit and knows when a good investment is in front of him. Starting with his family, people are his business and his chief concern. He consistently throws seed on good soil and invests his talents for a healthy increase. He has mentors and friends who advise him, and he is not too proud to ask for an honest opinion of himself. The Statesman is self-aware and continues to strive for improvement and life change. He recognizes God's hand in everything he sees, everything that happens, and every person he meets. He is the most complete man, yet he yearns for new challenges and growth.

The following statements will likely grab the Statesman's attention:

- The sky's the limit!
- What have you got to lose?
- Let's explore new possibilities!
- Let's do this together.
- With God, all things are possible.

Quick Takeaways for the Statesman Type:
1. Promises made are inviolable
2. Instead of stifling subordinates, he inspires them
3. His identity lies in who he is, not in what he can do or how he is viewed by others
4. He knows that other people are his chief concern in life

There is one additional area to address specifically for the Statesman: adversity. A man might do well with his words and deeds and be a person of integrity yet still encounter people with whom he strongly disagrees. Sometimes work associates or even friends and family can be hypercritical for no apparent reason. Despite this adversity, a Statesman keeps in mind the following three adversity rules:

- God uses and blesses people I disagree with.
- I can disagree with people without demonizing them to others.

- I can learn from critical people, knowing there may be some truth in what they are saying.

Before taking the Words and Deeds Diagnostic from chapter 3, many people might have guessed how they would score. But having character is fleshed out in the words and actions of a man, not simply in the way he perceives himself. If becoming a Statesman is something you desire, the later chapters of this book will provide a map for how to get there. But first, we must see the people we actually are, rooted in reality, and the Person who sets the standard for each of us. That is the focus of the following chapter.

CHAPTER 6

THE MASTER STATESMAN

Jesus is the most complete man.

JESUS IS DESCRIBED AS a man mighty in words and deeds (Luke 24:19). Was Jesus a Sentry, a Salesman, a Scout, or a Statesman?

No matter what can be said about Jesus, it is absolutely true that He had a lot of words for people, along with a lot of deeds. So we can immediately leave behind the idea that Jesus might have been a Sentry. But what kind of man was He? Was there synthesis in Jesus' life?

There is no doubt that Jesus did many, many good deeds. If one looks at the life of the man who started the Christian faith, they will immediately note the mighty deeds of His life. Jesus healed the sick, gave sight to the blind, and gave hearing to the deaf. Jesus made legs and backs straight and brought several people back to life. If that is not convincing enough, Jesus lived a sinless life, yet died to pay for the sin of humanity. It is recorded that on the third day, He rose again and walked and taught for weeks, when He was seen by hundreds of people.

There is also much evidence from Scripture that Jesus was a man of many good words that He shared with His first-century followers. The words of Christ can be categorized into three main parts: prophecy, teaching, and prayers. They continue to be studied, even memorized, today.

Did one area of Jesus' life overshadow the others? Let's take a closer look.

Teaching. Jesus instructed His listeners about many aspects of life: how to deal with relationships, how to deal with money, how to deal with enemies. Here are ten of the major directions Jesus gave His followers in the Sermon on the Mount (Matthew 5–7):

- Do not murder.
- Do not be angry at your brother.
- Do not commit adultery.
- Do not make oaths and vows.
- Do not seek your own revenge.
- Love not only your friends but your enemies.
- Do not give in order to be honored.
- Do not pray in order to be seen.
- Do not lay up treasures on earth.

- Do not be anxious about what you will eat and what you will wear.

When studying these edicts it is important to ask if Jesus practiced what He preached. Was Jesus a model when it came to His own teaching? Let's look at each of the ten edicts above through the lens of the historical record we know about Jesus' life.

Jesus was tried and convicted and executed—but not for murder. He was killed for making himself equal to God. Scripture records that He honored His mother throughout His adult life, and we do not have a record of Jesus being cross with any of His disciples. He spoke hard truths to them but was not angry or bitter toward them. He even rejected the logic of "an eye for an eye" as punishment for crime. He was angry at sin, especially the sins of those buying and selling in the Temple, but anger didn't characterize His relationships.

Did Jesus ever commit adultery? No. In fact, not only does the Bible describe every interaction Jesus had with the opposite sex as appropriate—the way a gentleman would treat a woman—the written biography of Jesus' life details how He affirmed and uplifted women, which was contrary to cultural norms.

We have no record of Jesus ever taking an oath or seeking revenge. And at the end of His life, instead of speaking an ill word toward those crucifying Him, Jesus prayed for them, that their sin would not be held against them. He forgave the unforgivable, loved the unlovable, and desired good for others, even when He was perishing.

Did Jesus store up treasures on earth, give in order to be honored, or pray in order to be seen? Scripture records that Jesus had Peter pay the Temple tax with a coin taken out of a fish's mouth, and Judas, not Jesus, managed the money box. Jesus was not a rich man; His sustenance was provided for on a daily basis. His currency was faith and healing or feeding those who might have expected material goods from Him.

As far as prayer, it is often recorded that Jesus went away to pray by Himself, usually in a remote area, while He and His disciples were away from the crowds. Jesus did not do things to glorify Himself.

Finally, was Jesus ever anxious? We know that Jesus had some intense moments before His arrest in Gethsemane. He prayed several times and asked God to remove that which was burdening Him. However, with the specific words that He taught about not worrying for one's daily provision, it is apparent that Jesus passes the test. Others around Jesus worried about what they would eat. His followers wondered how the multitudes would be fed. Jesus had perfect confidence that all would be provided from above. Never once does Scripture detail Jesus being concerned about clothing or his next meal. On the contrary, He summoned those who were concerned about those things to leave it all behind and follow Him. Those are not the words of someone who worried.

Jesus passes the test. His many good words are backed by His actions. So Jesus was not a Salesman or a Scout, and we have already established that He was not a Sentry. By our measure, He would be a Statesman. Please review these highlights of the Statesman and see how well they apply to Jesus.

- A Statesman is primarily focused on other people: He builds his life upon the bedrock of selfless service.
- His identity is fully formed, and he knows who he is.
- The Statesman is led by the Spirit and knows when a good investment is in front of him. Starting with his family, people are his business and his chief concern.
- The Statesman is self-aware and recognizes God's hand in everything he sees, everything that happens, and every person he meets.
- Instead of stifling subordinates, the Statesman inspires them.

Jesus was fully aware of His identity and mission on planet Earth. What He thought of Himself came into being: He would be sacrificed for the sins of the people. The crowds, however, and even His disciples believed something different about who Jesus was. His identity and mission as Messiah was not what the Jews expected, even if it was what they desperately needed. They thought they had a typical man on their hands, not the Son of God who was sent to save the world. Here is a graph that illustrates this point:

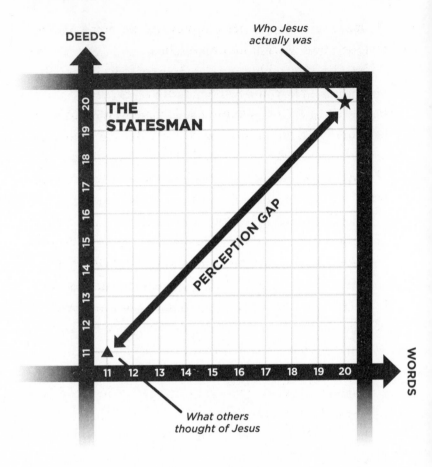

Even though there was a massive perception gap in Jesus' life with the way the Jews perceived Him, there was no real gap—nothing missing. Jesus was the complete man.

Jesus was a man of service, commitment, and strength. He inspired others with His words and actions. And even though His ministry was to the whole world, it did not end before He had taken care of His family first. In Jesus' dying breaths,

He made sure His mother was provided for by requesting that John treat Mary as his own mother.

Jesus knew who He was, what His mission would accomplish, and how God was working behind the scenes in every event to be glorified in Christ's actions. Jesus was not on a haphazard mission, thrown together in a desperate moment because nothing else would work. He was intentional with His words and His deeds. He followed a master plan that would achieve the greatest results.

No one in history has ever fully understood the depths of the human condition or the reasons for human behavior except Jesus. The human soul is much more wicked, cunning, and insidious than we can ever imagine. Yet the love of God stands ready to meet all of the evil—including all of our own personal evil—with forgiveness, acceptance, and freedom.

The next chapter directly relates to what Jesus was sent to accomplish for us. Every man must be willing to address the gaps in his life and lean into the things that will help him live well—desires of a true Statesman.

CHAPTER 7

THE GAP

I am doing the very thing I hate!

MARTIN WORKED AT a large computer software company where promotions had been steady. One of the things he enjoyed about working there was that each time he was promoted, Martin received a nicer office, more responsibility, and a larger team of people to lead. With his last promotion, however, his new team was expecting someone else—one of their own—to be their director, not Martin. They did not receive the new boss as warmly as Martin desired.

One person in particular always challenged Martin's authority: Bruce, a long-standing employee who most of the others felt should have received Martin's position. Whatever Martin said to the team, Bruce had a sarcastic quip that would make a few coworkers chuckle. Martin could see them talk about him after work meetings. He noticed how stiff everyone around Bruce would become when Martin walked by. This behavior kept Martin awake at night.

How was he supposed to lead a team when half of the group didn't respect his authority? The situation seemed hopeless. Then Martin had an idea. What if he were to have a party at his place and show them that he was truly a great guy? Perhaps Bruce would find a reason not to come, which was Martin's desire.

Martin made all the preparations. Finally, the big day arrived, and people from his directorate came to his house for appetizers and dessert. Even Bruce came, much to Martin's chagrin.

Things were going well until Martin told a story in the kitchen. Just before Martin got to the punch line, Bruce sauntered in. Immediately, Martin noticed how everyone froze up. Unfortunately, Martin let it get to him and the punch line faltered. People slipped away without much of a response, and Martin began seething inside.

Everyone left except Bruce, who stood by the counter and stared at Martin.

"Do you have something you want to say, Bruce?" asked Martin, a little indignantly.

"Well, great story, but I'm sad I missed the first part of it," Bruce said, with a smirk.

"I'm sure you are," responded Martin. "Listen, what do you want from me? I can tell you don't respect my leadership, but do you have to make things miserable for both of us?"

"I'm not miserable," said Bruce. "I'm disappointed about the job, and I think Human Resources hired the wrong person—but I'm not miserable. I know it's just a matter of time until you mess up, and then they will need someone else to step in, just like what happened to the last guy."

"Did you make things difficult for your last director as well?" Martin asked.

"I wouldn't say so. I could see his obvious faults before everyone else could, but soon they could see them too."

Martin was seeing a larger picture now: It was not just him; it was the entire system Bruce was sabotaging. For the good of the company, Martin felt he should do something about it.

"Look, Bruce, it is evident that the company doesn't want you in my position. You had several chances, but each time, they chose someone else. You obviously have talent, but the company doesn't want you in leadership."

Martin knew his words would sting Bruce a little, but it felt good to say them anyway.

"That's fine," said Bruce, nodding his head a little with intensity in his green eyes.

Just then, another employee, Francisco, walked into the kitchen. Francisco was a nice person, congenial and pleasant around everyone.

"Oh, hey, guys, how's it going?" Francisco asked nervously, surprised to see Martin and Bruce alone talking.

"Hey, Francisco, I have a question for you," Martin said. "Tell us something: Who do you think is a better leader, Bruce or I?"

"This is crazy," said Bruce, making motions to leave the room.

"No, it's not," said Martin, motioning with his hands for Bruce to stay. "I just want an honest point of view here—I think it would help both of us."

"Well, I don't really know; you're both really capable people," muttered Francisco.

"I realize that," said Martin. "We just want to know who you think has better leadership skills, Bruce or I?"

Francisco froze, unable to say anything. To his relief, the door opened again and Sarah, Martin's assistant, walked into the kitchen.

"There you two are. People are wondering what happened to you," said Sarah, smiling at both Bruce and Martin.

Martin began again. "Sarah, we're having a little contest. Tell us, who do you think is a better director? I mean, we all know that Bruce hasn't had a chance yet, but if he were the director, who do you think would make better decisions, Bruce or I?" asked Martin.

Sarah looked around the room. Bruce had an awful grin on his face, and Francisco had his head down, trying not to make eye contact with anyone.

"Oh, boss, this is really awkward, you know," said Sarah. "I can't choose between you two. I mean, Bruce has worked here a long time, and I know his kids. And you're, well, you're our director. You shouldn't make people choose between you."

The door opened again, and it was Cal, Bruce's long-standing friend. Martin had seen those two snicker about him numerous times. Bruce could always get a laugh out of Cal, and Martin never could. Cal was very competent and Martin respected him, but Cal couldn't have been a worse candidate, due to his friendship with Bruce. Yet Martin figured he did not have anything to lose. He was already treading on thin ice and emotionally worked up, so why not get to the bottom of this once and for all?

"Hey, Cal, glad you could stop in. We were just having a friendly discussion about leadership. Some think Bruce would be a better director than I would, and some are happy with who is in charge now. I will not tell you who said what, so just answer honestly. Who do you think has better leadership skills, Bruce or I?"

Martin was a little edgy engaging Cal so forcefully. He looked down at the counter and found some peanuts, which he jammed into his mouth out of nervousness.

Cal looked around the room and noticed Bruce grin and give a slight wink to him. He then looked at Francisco and Sarah, with heads down, obviously embarrassed at being put on the spot like this by their director.

Cal felt a little out of place to address the issue in Martin's kitchen but decided to engage Martin's question head-on because he was disgusted with the divisiveness in the directorate.

"It's an interesting question, Martin, but before I answer it, I have a few of my own questions for you. First off, did you know much about our division when you applied for the position, or did you look up some facts on Google before you came in for the interview? Also, besides this party—which isn't going very well, by the way—what have you done to build our team and bring trust to the group? Last, do you really think it's an appropriate use of your authority to make your employees choose between you and someone else at an office social engagement?"

Martin shook his head a little bit, wondering what had just happened. The momentum turned on him, and it seemed someone sucked all the oxygen out of the room. Cal, Bruce, Francisco, and Sarah stood still and silent, staring at Martin and wondering what he was going to say. Finally, Bruce broke the silence.

"Well, this has been a fun little exercise," Bruce said. "It looks like our leader is now at a loss for words. I better go mingle. Cheers."

Bruce left, Cal left, Francisco left, and Sarah was walking out but turned and pressed her lips together while considering what she should say. Martin looked up at her like a whipped pup, hoping she could say something to inspire him.

"You know what?" Sarah finally said. "Bruce is not such a bad guy, once you get to know him. Perhaps you should make more of an effort." Sarah then turned and walked out.

A rebuke from a trusted subordinate! Sarah's words couldn't have stung more, because Martin considered her his only ally. His own assistant now pitied the very person Martin was trying to show up. *Things couldn't be worse*, thought Martin.

Just then, Martin heard loud laughter from the living room. It was Bruce, telling another story. Martin cracked the kitchen door a little so he could peek out. Bruce had the entire party circled around and was unraveling a fascinating story about his last vacation. Martin didn't know what to do or where to go. Even in his own house, Bruce controlled the space and had him trapped in the kitchen. *Is it hot in here, or is it just me?* Martin wondered. He grabbed some more peanuts and jammed them into his mouth, chewing furiously.

*   *   *   *

Martin and Bruce both have what I call a gap in their lives. A "gap" is a break in continuity between two objects. For men, and for the purposes of this book, the gap is the distance between where a man currently is with his integrity and where he wants to be. Some men took the test in chapter 3 thinking they were already strong Statesmen, but their scores reveal them to be Sentries, Salesmen, or Scouts. It can be challenging to take an assessment like the one in this book. No one sets out to live a life lacking in integrity; most of us aspire to live well and have a positive impact on the world. And yet, an assessment like this one exposes our vulnerabilities. We're not the Statesmen we thought we were; there's a deficit in our words, our deeds, or the integration of the two.

To continue living in this sort of denial will give a man persistent blind spots. No man wants to end his life with regret, knowing he could have bridged the integrity gap but never tried. This book was written to help men confront who they are now and become who they want to be in the future. The good news is that the gap is easily crossed, once a man decides he is ready to change.

Discovering the gap between where a man currently is and where he desires to be should make the man feel somewhat uncomfortable and vulnerable. Even as a Statesman, there is an annoying gap, because no one is perfect. There is always room for improvement. The apostle Paul was a Statesman—his words have shaped civilization over the course of millennia, and his deeds included helping launch the worldwide Christian movement—and yet, even he recognized a gap in his life: "What I am doing, I do not understand; for I am not practicing what I would like to do, but I am doing the very thing I hate" (Romans 7:15). For the purposes of this study, I call this personal integrity gap the *primary gap*.

There is another gap to address, and I call it the *perception gap*. The perception gap is that area of our inner world excluded from our awareness; the perceived words and deeds of a man as he sees himself versus the words and deeds of the man actually experienced by others. This gap is what others believe to be true about a man, even though he himself may not see it or believe it to be true. In the story of Martin and Bruce, it was easy for Martin's coworkers to see the self-confidence challenges in his life, but much harder for him to do so. It is scary for most men to ponder what others might know about them that they do not perceive about themselves. I've wondered about this area in my own life. *Am I missing something important? Do I have an issue everyone else sees in me that I cannot see for myself? What if it is negative and I am unintentionally hurting those around me?*

Our perception gaps usually consist of a mixture of two or more blind spots:

- A lack of listening to other people
- A lack of caring for other people
- An inability to take the focus of conversation off self
- An inability to see how comments negatively impact others
- A tendency to embellish stories, particularly to uplift self
- A tendency to sound like a know-it-all, or to come across as holier-than-thou
- A tendency to think your time schedule is the only one that matters

Men sometimes know when they are being rude or short with someone and continue to do it intentionally for effect. The above list, however, can happen in the fog of unawareness, and men may not perceive when they convey a sense of selfishness to others. To succeed in this life, self-awareness is crucially important; thus, the reason for the inventory in this book.

In order to go further and face reality head-on, I challenge every man reading this book to allow three other people to take the online Words and Deeds Diagnostic as it pertains to him. Use family members, good friends, or daily work associates, but try to have a mixture. For instance, I would ask my wife, my supervisor at work, and a longtime friend. People who see you in action every day have the best vantage point by which to evaluate your life, and they will appraise you differently than you appraise yourself. Asking other men to weigh in on the state of your character will not be easy. It will take additional time, energy, and vulnerability, but it can bring some highly valuable self-awareness into your life and perhaps enlighten some decades-old blind spots.

The composite score of the three friends who take the survey for you will give you a good idea where others see you. Again, this is called the *perception gap*. The goal is *not* to achieve the highest score possible but to attain maximum self-understanding. As we learned from Captain Sims in chapter 2, "Professionalism requires a constant personal net assessment." And as Proverbs 27:17 declares, "As iron sharpens iron, so one person sharpens another" (NIV).

MY SCORES

Friend #1	Words _____	Deeds _____
Friend #2	Words _____	Deeds _____
Friend #3	Words _____	Deeds _____
Total Score (add all 3)	Words _____	Deeds _____
Average (divide by 3)	Words _____	Deeds _____

Compare the average from your friends' assessment to your own assessment: Words _____ Deeds _____.

For clarity, the two gaps addressed so far are the *primary gap*—the gap between where a man has scored and where he wants to be—and the *perception gap*—the gap between where a man thinks he is and where he actually is based on an external assessment. The first instance is a man's comprehension or *his own* grasping of his shortfalls. The second instance is a man's lack of understanding of the reality *others perceive* about his shortfalls.

- The Primary Gap → A man's comprehension of his own shortfalls
- The Perception Gap → A man's incomprehension of how others perceive him

These gaps are outlined in the diagram below.

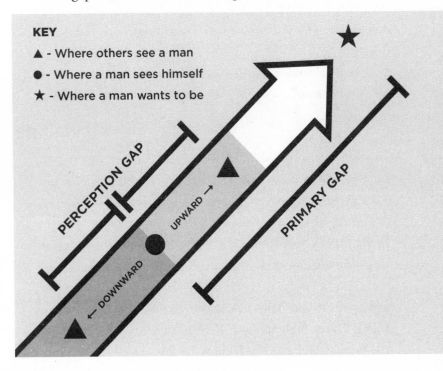

KEY

▲ - Where others see a man
● - Where a man sees himself
★ - Where a man wants to be

PERCEPTION GAP

UPWARD →

← DOWNWARD

PRIMARY GAP

Imagine a man took his own questionnaire with a score of 14 for words and a score of 6 for deeds. He knows there is a primary gap between his current position (Salesman) and where he wants to be (Statesman). Then he has three work associates take the test for him, and a composite of their results totals a score of 6 for his words and a score of 6 for his deeds. He has a *downward* perception gap (14 versus 6). This is displayed in the diagram on the next page.

As a rule, a man should not be troubled with *upward* perception gaps (where his friends score him higher than he scores himself), nor let them go to his head. However, primary gaps coupled with *downward* perception gaps should be looked at right away. Please fill out the short exercise below.

My Primary Gap(s):   Words   or   Deeds   or   Both
My Perception Gap(s): Words   or   Deeds   or   Both

* * * *

Why are there gaps? Why do we have to experience life with breaches in our integrity and a lack of perception into how we come across to others? Some might say we are misinformed or lacking training. Some might assume we are lazy or apathetic. We might have had a tough upbringing or a sour relationship in adulthood. Whatever the reasons we come up with, they are merely excuses—or, better put, symptoms of our main disease: our sinful nature. As St. Paul put it, "Wretched man that I am! Who will set me free from the body of this death?" (Romans 7:24).

Having a blind spot is not detrimental in itself, but it can contribute to a relationship crisis if not eventually dealt with. Self-awareness is the key to avoiding a blind spot. The more we consider linking our words and our deeds, the fewer

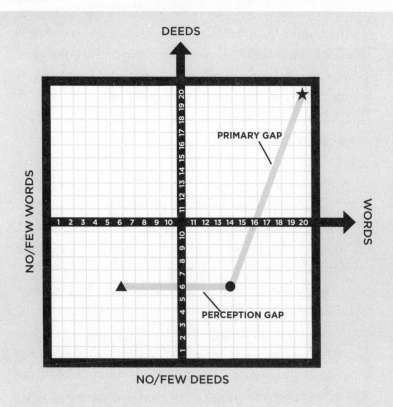

KEY

▲ - Where others see a man

● - Where a man sees himself

★ - Where a man wants to be

blind spots we will have. Let us not be like the old codger who declares he will never change, that people must accept him for who he is. People like that have a trail of tears in their past relationships.

As men, we have tremendous expectations put on us by our employers, spouses, families, churches, and sometimes our neighbors or landlords. Life is not easy. Sometimes these expectations are unmanageable. Sometimes we have expectations of ourselves that are unmanageable.

If you're feeling worn out and need a break, ask yourself some questions:

- When is your job good enough?
- When is your marriage good enough?
- When is your relationship with your kids good enough?

We don't often think in those terms; we just feel awash in setbacks, like the gap will never be filled. But this is not the case. We simply need to allow our words to match our deeds, and then we can be adequate for any task at hand.

After Paul throws up his arms because of his sense of his own depravity, he states, "There is therefore now no condemnation for those who are in Christ Jesus" (Romans 8:1, ESV).

There is hope. Although there are many things in life we cannot control, we know that there is Someone in control of human events.

Some men do not believe that true success in life and relationships is possible on this side of heaven, but they are mistaken. When our words and deeds are wise and aligned, then our primary gap and perception gaps evaporate. Success becomes possible. Relationships are restored. There is hope— and not a shallow hope, but a hope that does not disappoint. Peace and wholeness come into our lives as we live out the truths we believe.

But beware—there are several land mines we men must avoid.

The Reason for Gaps: Integrity Terrorists

You have declared yourself in the battle for integrity. There are three thieves, terrorists that will attack your integrity, seeking to destroy all the good you have achieved in your life. They are subtle—we can live with these thieves for years without awareness—but they are quietly and deeply sapping us. Like a hidden explosive device on a route recon, their deadly potential lies unnoticed until it is too late.

Pride (Arrogance)

Is your integrity ever terrorized by a low humility? The English word *pride* is associated with the Latin word *superbia*. Technically, it means an inordinate satisfaction derived from one's achievements—self-esteem to the level that one looks down on others, or an unreasonable conceit about one's talents. The problem with pride is enormous.

First, for believers, pride displays a lack of belief. The nature of God's grace is that we cannot achieve a moral justification for our own existence, nor can we achieve enough righteousness for God to overlook the depth of our sin. Only the substitution of Christ's righteousness for our own—through his atoning death on a cross—fits us for eternal life with God. If we truly believe this (and it is the basis of the Christian faith), there is no place for pride in our own accomplishments, because these achievements will not get us to heaven.

Because of our sin and our desperate need for salvation, we cannot look down on others. We all need God. We all need Christ's forgiveness. The struggle with pride is essentially a struggle with unbelief. To indulge in pride is to denounce the simple gospel message, to remove God from His rightful place. Proud men take God's rightful worship and are ever needy for more praise from other humans. True believers are satisfied knowing God loves them, and man's praise is hollow. Thus, confession—not bragging—demonstrates faith for believers.

Second, pride can deceive us into thinking that we *are actually better* than other people. Proud people believe their opinions are the best, their personalities are the best, and their decisions are the ones everyone should not only agree with but also praise. People suffering with pride have an enormous capacity for deception. No praise, honor, or admiration is too great for them. Those with pride become the center of everything. When others say something, the person with pride interprets the conversation as all about him. Benjamin Franklin stated that men wrapped up in themselves make very small packages, and this is very true. When we are self-focused, our effectiveness in every area of life is hindered.

Ultimately, a man lacking in self-awareness and steeped in pride will inflict pain on everyone around him. He will find himself in competition with others. Instead of simply doing his best, a proud man has to *be* the best at all costs, even if it lowers those around him. It is lost on him that greatness in the Kingdom is based on servanthood, suffering, and humility—traits in direct opposition to what pride seeks to gain.[1]

Third, pride can make us believe we are the captains of our own ships. No position or place for us is so great that it guarantees our future. There is also no position so small that God does not see. He is the captain of our ships. He is in charge of whether we are raised or lowered. We are to accept every promotion or difficulty from His hand with similar grace and acceptance.

Many jealousies in the workplace and even at church have to do with wanting to be someone we are not. A man not blinded by pride understands what his role is and is more concerned with impacting others than with being rewarded for every good deed; he knows he is ultimately rewarded by God, and this gives him a calm assurance. He knows that when the team wins, he wins.

The mythological story of Narcissus is a lesson on the danger of self-absorption. As the story goes, the hunter Narcissus was proud of his beauty and disdained those who loved him. Tired of his arrogance, the gods lured him to a pool where, upon seeing his reflection, Narcissus instantly fell in love with his image and refused to ever leave. Choosing to stare at his beauty above all else, Narcissus eventually lost his will to live.

An arrogant man has enormous capacity for self-deception; unfortunately, he never sees it. He chooses to make his life an idol instead of investing it to help others. Others perceive that the man's life is all about him—as the gods did with Narcissus—and quickly tire of his company. The man foolishly accepts that his greatest interest should be in himself.

> A man's pride will bring him low,
> But a humble spirit will obtain honor.
>
> PROVERBS 29:23

Lying (Deceit)

Lying inherently violates the value of being a man of your word. A lie is an untruth. Some men struggle with lying because they like to mince words to give themselves some wiggle room; what they say dances right around the truth. Some call that a white lie. Other men lie outright. Those with integrity are always caught by surprise when they hear that someone told an outright lie. How could he do it? Has he no moral code?

The reasons for lying are numerous. A well-timed fib can alleviate a problem, at least in the short term. Little Johnny learned this in grade school when his teacher asked him if he did his homework. If he answered no, there were immediate consequences; if he answered yes, it delayed his teacher's wrath and he had a fifty-fifty chance of going unnoticed.

Even as adults, we depend on probabilities for getting away with small fibs. When we text folks and tell them we are on our way when we have not yet gotten into our cars or we say we took care of something but it was not fully performed, we are doing the same thing as Johnny, playing the odds that we will probably not get caught.

This kind of behavior poses a big problem. People are not our number one audience—God is, and He sees all. Lying and fibbing shows a great lack of respect for not only the person we are offending but also the Person controlling our destiny. When we recognize that God's presence is always with us, then we can no longer tell others anything but the truth, because lying to others is essentially lying to God, who hears all.

Lying terrorizes and steals from our integrity because it puts self first, even before God. It shows no true concern or love for the other person because it does not give them an authentic view of who we are. Fractioning off the truth fractions off part of our lives, and we remain incomplete people. No wholeness exists in our relationships when lying is involved.

> A lying tongue hates those it crushes,
> And a flattering mouth works ruin.
> PROVERBS 26:28

Lust (Envy)

Lust is a common topic in books for men, but the broader category and focus of this discussion is envy over what we do not currently possess. To be envious means to have a feeling of discontentment or resentfulness because of what someone else has gained. Such comparison is an integrity killer. If we are not content with ourselves for who we are, then we will not be content with what we have.

True Statesmen are satisfied with their lot in life. It is not that they do not perform their best and move forward, but that they work to succeed out of a sense of joyful experience, not because someone else has it better than them. To work at something merely to attain what someone else has achieved is empty and unsatisfying. This goes back to calling. What have you been called to do? We find more purpose in keeping our eyes on the ball in our own field of play than in pursuing someone else's dream, calling, or position. How or why God positions other men should not be our chief concern in life.

C. S. Lewis wrote to a friend, Arthur Greeves, on September 12, 1933, about how sometimes in our longings we do not believe God wants the best for us and think that we know better than Him what direction to take.

> Supposing you are taking a dog on a lead through a turnstile or past a post. You know what happens (apart from his usual ceremonies in passing a post!). He tries to go the wrong side and gets his lead looped round the post. *You* see that he can't do it, and therefore pull him back. You pull him *back* because you want to enable him to go *forward*. He wants exactly the same thing—namely to go *forward*: for that very reason he resists your pull *back*, or, if

he is an obedient dog, yields to it reluctantly as a matter of duty which seems to him to be quite in opposition to his own will: tho' *in fact* it is only by yielding to you that he will ever succeed in getting where he wants.[2]

We humans long for happiness. But the reality is, most people seek it in directions that are ultimately not fulfilling. When we lust for what we do not have, we buy into the lie that what *we* want for ourselves is better than what God wants for our lives. Lewis went on to write the following:

God not only understands but *shares* the desire which is at the root of all my evil—the desire for complete and ecstatic happiness. He made me for no other purpose than to enjoy it. But He knows, and I do not, how it can be really and permanently attained. He knows that most of *my* personal attempts to reach it are actually putting it further and further out of my reach.[3]

This is actually very freeing. We can rest in the security that God is in control of our lives. We do not need to be concerned with how someone else is operating. Perhaps a friend of yours scored as a Statesman on his diagnostic and you scored as a Sentry. Should you be envious? The short answer is *no*. You have no idea how someone else operates on a day-to-day basis and how honestly he assessed himself.

And even if the results are accurate, you should be thankful for the mirror to see a broader picture of yourself. We should always strive for improvement, to be better in God's eyes, but this striving is an individual concern, not a quest to be better than someone else.

When we are men of integrated words and deeds, our lives are aligned around the right things. Our relationships are healthy and helpful to others. They are not based on quid pro quo (this for that). Men of integrity intuitively know that they do not need to envy things they currently do not have. All they truly need is taken care of by the Lord. Contentment—being happy with the life the Lord has provided—is the key here.

If the reader will have patience for one more illustration about a dog, here is a short fable from Aesop about contentment:

> Once there was a dog who happily came upon a juicy piece of meat as he was running alongside a rapidly flowing river. When the dog glanced into the river, he saw his own reflection firmly holding the piece of meat in his teeth. Mistaking the reflection for another dog with something better, he opened his mouth to snatch it and ended up losing what he had when it dropped into the water.[4]

How many men, like the dog, have reached out for what they thought would make them happy, only to realize they have now steered off course, that what they saw was a mirage? Men, there will always be things about your life you wish you could change. But accepting the life the Lord has given to you is the first step to true happiness.

> A tranquil heart gives life to the flesh,
>   but envy makes the bones rot.
> PROVERBS 14:30, ESV

Not all men struggle with one of the three integrity terrorists listed above. There are other vices, including anger, slothfulness, greed, and gluttony. When any of these terrorists overcomes a human heart, it takes its owner far away from the heart of Christianity. Thankfully, there are words and deeds that can boost our integrity and re-place Christ in the center of our lives. That is the focus of the next chapter.

CHAPTER 8

FORCE MULTIPLIERS

Tell me I have led a good life.

ONE OF THE MOST POIGNANT movie scenes I know of is from *Saving Private Ryan*. Aged World War II veteran James Ryan turns to his wife from a graveside at the Normandy American Cemetery and Memorial in France. "Tell me I have led a good life," he says. "Tell me I'm a good man."[1] The film had opened with Ryan walking with his family through the cemetery in search of a specific marker. When he found it, he collapsed to his knees, overcome with emotion. Immediately, the film transitions to an epic portrayal of the assault on Omaha Beach on June 6, 1944, and continues with a team of army rangers tasked with finding Ryan, the last surviving brother in his family. After the rangers find Private Ryan, they undergo hand-to-hand combat in a small town where nearly the entire team is killed. In his final words, their dying captain tells Ryan, "Earn this. Earn it!"

When someone gives their life for you, you are compelled to make your life count. Ryan wanted to know that the other soldiers had invested their lives into something meaningful by saving him. In a larger sense, this is what a nation's military defense does collectively, putting their lives in jeopardy so that others might live a good life.

This is also the message of Christianity.

*   *   *   *

A term frequently utilized in combat is *force multiplier*. It refers to an attribute that significantly increases the effectiveness of the group to accomplish its mission. A force multiplier amplifies a system's contributing parts to produce greater than expected results. It can be a piece of technology, a tool, a weapon—even the weather sometimes multiplies the effect a fighting unit can have on its enemy.

When it comes to integrity, the following six activities are force multipliers.

Prayer

Think about a force multiplier in combat—perhaps a bunker buster bomb, which has the capacity to penetrate ten feet of concrete and hit the enemy where they think they are safe. That is what prayer is.

Prayer is *Star Wars*, a high-tech defense system. It is the air force performing offensive operations on situations the army could not impact on its own. Prayer is taking God at His word and trusting Him. Prayer is acknowledging that God cares about all the little things in life and knowing that He is in charge.

Complacency is the biggest hurdle in relation to prayer. We have to remind ourselves often that what we cannot see is more real, truer than what we can see. This is hard, but the more we develop a reliance on prayer in our private lives, the more it will rub off on us during the rest of the day. We are weak creatures and fight against discipline, yet there is much joy in spending time talking with God. Some days will be dry (prayer-wise), and that's okay. Combining prayer—for yourself and others—with Bible study and worship is particularly helpful, as is kneeling while praying. Prayer is vital in fighting the spiritual battle.

Forgiveness

Police officer Steven McDonald died the day I wrote this chapter. McDonald was a New York City cop shot in his neck, wrist, and face by a young man named Shavod "Buddha" Jones in 1986.[2] McDonald was left paralyzed from the neck down. At the time, his wife was pregnant with their first child. At his son's baptism, McDonald stunned the world by announcing that he completely forgave his shooter and hoped Jones could find peace in his life.

A Christian bishop who spoke to McDonald while he was in the hospital impacted the police officer's view of his tragic situation. The bishop told McDonald that Jesus didn't save the world through teaching and miracles; He did it lying motionless on His back. McDonald went on to speak all over the United States, a living, broken example of forgiveness and peace after tragedy.

We men know what it means to be bitter toward someone. We all have people in our lives who have crossed us and never apologized. Some have done it out of carelessness. Others have intentionally stepped on us out of spite. A man might have a close family member who has hurt him, physically or emotionally, and it is desperately hard not to hold a grudge against that person. Bitterness can be a deadly antagonist to our integrity. *We cannot be men of words and deeds and hold a grudge against someone.*

Who, right now, is on the dartboard of your mind? Who has hurt you to such an extent that you not only feel disinclined to forgive them but also think they should *pay* for what they have done to you? Scripture speaks often about this unwillingness to forgive. One verse that is very clear on this topic is Matthew 6:14-15: "If you forgive other people when they sin against you, your heavenly Father will also forgive you. But if you do not forgive others their sins, your Father will not forgive your sins" (NIV). This is a sobering verse; it holds both a promise and a warning.

Forgiveness is not letting someone off the hook. It is not forgetting. It is not an emotion or a feeling. Forgiveness is an action, a step we take because we love another person. It is the willing surrender of resentment and of any right to get even. It is allowing others to be accountable to God for their actions and allowing ourselves to love them regardless.

Forgiveness is unilateral. Romans 12:19 declares, "Beloved, never avenge yourselves, but leave it to the wrath of God, for it is written, 'Vengeance is mine, I will repay, says the Lord'"(ESV).

Forgiveness is a unique convergence of words and deeds. It doesn't take place without the word *forgiveness*, but it is actualized in the actions of the forgiver. That might involve reconciliation with a person who wronged you—"I forgive you, and I look forward to being in fellowship with you again." Or, where reconciliation is impossible or irresponsible—"I forgive him, and now I'll no longer be paralyzed by the hurt he caused me." It's possible that the first step out of life as a Sentry is to forgive the person or people who have caused you to shut down. With forgiveness, a man can move forward—like McDonald—and encourage the world that there is life after tragedy.

Active Listening

Is listening to those around you difficult for you? Join the club. Listening is tough for nearly every man I have met. To be *in* the moment is hard for most of us men because we are usually trying to think one or two steps ahead of the current conversation. In a world where people regularly forget to listen to one another, a Statesman changes the world by listening to it.

Listening to others when they are communicating with us is our gift to them. It communicates to others how important they are to us. And when we listen and then answer with a loving response, that combination of words and deeds is a double gift.

Frequently people share with us just because they need to be heard; they do not expect or even want a solution from us. Empathy and understanding? Yes. Solutions? Not necessarily. We can give someone a gift of our time by the simple activity of listening. Conversely, we can hurt someone by not listening. Proverbs 18:13 declares, "To answer before listening—that is folly and shame" (NIV). We will never love deeply without pausing our lives when someone tries to speak to us.[3]

How does a man remember to stay in the moment? For me, it is by forcibly telling myself to pay attention. I remind myself to focus on what they are saying. The script going through my head at the moment someone begins speaking to me is "Pay attention, pay attention, pay attention." I don't always get this right, and I regret it when I have to ask someone to repeat something they just said. The expression on the other's face says it all.

Intently listening to someone else is a force multiplier because it communicates the importance of that person and builds their sense of self-worth. We may not all know the exact thing to say to others when they are going through something heavy, but a listening ear can build an important bridge to the relationship and help mend another's heart.

Promptness

Promptess probably seems odd on a list of force multipliers for integrity. However, promptness is somewhat like listening: It gives another person the gift of our presence.

A lot has been written on why people are late. Some are trying to get as much done as possible and keep working right up to the last minute. This good intention does not absolve them of their problem, however, and usually the offender is completely oblivious that being late impacts others. Some who struggle with promptness are not trying to maximize their productivity, but they simply have a hard time leaving in order to get somewhere on time. My father-in-law used to tell his family, "You can't leave the house when you are supposed to be somewhere and be on time!" How many people are frustrated with someone in their life who constantly runs late? Many. But this section is written for those who are late themselves.

Promptness boosts your integrity, and lateness destroys it.[4] You simply cannot be late to certain events and be considered a man of integrity. Athletic games start on time. Rocket launches, military formations, interviews, funerals, weddings, and church services all have times that must be adhered to. It is a common occurrence for employees to ask a boss for more time to complete a project, for students to ask teachers for an extension of a deadline, and for researchers to explain the need for more time to their directors. When we are supposed to be at work by 8 a.m, our supervisors expect us to have our toes under our desks at 8 a.m. But this is hard for some of us men.

Like listening, being on time is an expression of respect and deference toward other people. We make an extra effort not to put others out. Promptness, then, is a way to win people's hearts. People have been let down by many in this area, so showing up on time automatically reveals their importance to us and elevates their opinion of our character.

Resiliency

I like to call resiliency "stick-to-it-ness." It is the ability to persevere even when your heart and mind cannot perceive a clear and successful path ahead. Resiliency contains more than the old phrase *Just let it roll off your back*, which suggests that the injustice does not affect you; if not dealt with appropriately, its wound might be nursed indefinitely and garner thoughts that lead to bitterness and brokenness.

Resiliency is more than just *ignoring* something. It is moving through the pain, the emotions, the heartache, or the sheer stupidity of something without compromising one's integrity. There is still truth-telling. There is still admission of pain and frustration. And there can even be a call for help. But resiliency is about *will* in a man's life that is directed by something higher than himself, and it moves through darkness, defeat, and even success with a steady hand. A resilient man may experience defeat in one arena, but he doesn't take out his frustration on other arenas in his life. He continues to measure his words and carefully consider his actions.

During the war in Iraq, and especially the 2007 surge of troops, the military began to realize that resiliency is what was needed from men and women who serve. They subsequently began to promote it, saying that the resilient soldier has the mental fortitude to be successful in combat. The only problem is that men cannot produce this internal spring from nothing; there must be something outside themselves, a fountain to draw strength from. Many men in combat move forward to accomplish their mission but remain empty wells, and the results are seen when they return home to their families. They let issues roll off their backs until their unreplenished souls are wounded, and then PTSD becomes their reality.

But there is a higher way. Where does the strength come from for a man to see his way home and to be there for his friends and family? It doesn't come from the mental capacities within but from without; it comes from God. What matters most is not the measure of our strength but the source of our strength. In the Gospel of Matthew, Jesus tells His followers to come to Him when they are weary and burdened and that He will give them rest (Matthew 11:28). The Gospel of John has Jesus tell His followers that if they abide in Him, they will bear much fruit (John 15:5). When we truly admit our weakness and inabilities to Christ, He supplies us with strength, gifts, wisdom, and the fruit of the Spirit—all things we could never acquire without Him. Only the resilient man can tap into this reservoir of the triune Godhead and drink deeply from wells of peace and patience and perseverance, and only he can move forward and be a lighthouse for those potential shipwrecks around him.

A final note on resiliency: This is how we overcome cowardice as well. When we encounter times of weakness and fear, we may simultaneously recognize God's power, which is still in full effect in our lives. It is often in our struggles and trials that we can sense Him steering us. King David declared that though an army encamped around him, he would not fear, because the Lord was his stronghold and salvation (Psalm 27:1-3). The more we understand God's presence, even amidst the least likely circumstances, the more we become resilient, strong, and fearless.

Kindness

The elemental experience of love in human relationships is kindness. When we are kind to others, it shows a degree of character, compassion, and civility that is often lacking in our society. When I speak of being kind, I mean someone who is generous, patient, warmhearted, helpful, or thoughtful. Kindness is performing an act of love without expecting anything in return. One cannot earn kindness because kindness can only be given freely. Proverbs 19:22 reminds us, "What is desirable in a man is his kindness." Kindness is a huge integrity force multiplier. It allows people to see a man more interested in others than he is in himself.

Kindness is sometimes overlooked by those writing about love. However, kindness should be considered love's DNA, or love's volcanic core. Interestingly, the word used in the Old Testament to describe God's love, *hesed*, is translated as "loving-kindness."[5] It means goodness, kindness, and devotion. The word for love used for Jesus' teaching is *agapao*.[6] This word means predominantly three things: to have a warm regard for and interest in another person, to have high esteem for or satisfaction in something, or to practice or express love (or prove one's love). *Caritas* is the Latin translation of *agape*; from it comes the English word *charity*.

Kindness is a significant force multiplier in relationships. In marriage, for example, it can cement a bond of trust and friendship with your marriage partner. Unfortunately, sometimes a man can be kinder to a stranger he just met than he is to his own spouse. When a husband says he loves his wife but then is not kind to her, I know there is a misunderstanding of the word *love*. One can be kind without being in love, but one cannot be in love without being kind. Love is an incredibly important part of life, and Scripture tells us that we are indeed nothing without love (1 Corinthians 13:2; 1 John 4:7-21). When we reject pride, when we forgive, when we are prompt and present in our relationships, when we tell the truth even when it hurts to do so, when we pray for others and reject envy, we are displaying love and kindness, which is the way God designed us to live.

* * * *

Remember how the dying captain tells Private Ryan to "earn this. Earn it!"? The six character qualities in this chapter can help us maximize our time here on earth, but they are only a start. There are certainly other world-impacting force multipliers, and they all culminate in—and emanate from—the foundational force multiplier: our faith.

He is my steadfast love and my fortress,
my stronghold and my deliverer,
my shield and he in whom I take refuge,
who subdues peoples under me.

PSALM 144:2, ESV

CHAPTER 9

YOU AS STATESMAN

. . . but if not, O king . . .

WHO ARE YOU? This question is not about the job you are currently doing. Who are you really? Coming to grips with your own identity is an important step in the journey of a man. We all wear different hats: father, husband, brother, son, laborer, neighbor, churchman, and so on. But deep inside, there is an essence that is not defined by our titles. Beyond what we do, our thoughts and beliefs about ourselves will form a picture of the men we think we are.

I have always been inspired by the story of Martin Luther King Jr., an African American pastor and civil rights leader. King developed a reputation of using nonviolent protests to kick America's conscience. He was even insulted by other members of the black community—like Malcolm X—for not using enough force to create change, yet King's peaceful methods ultimately proved more effective than those of his violent contemporaries.

Some of King's most inspiring words came when he was sitting in a Birmingham jail in April 1963 after one of his nearly thirty arrests. His letter to fellow clergy declared,

> I hope the church as a whole will meet the challenge of this decisive hour. But even if the church does not come to the aid of justice, I have no despair about the future. I have no fear about the outcome of our struggle in Birmingham, even if our motives are at present misunderstood. We will reach the goal of freedom in Birmingham and all over the nation, because the goal of America is freedom. Abused and scorned though we may be, our destiny is tied up with America's destiny. . . . If the inexpressible cruelties of slavery could not stop us, the opposition we now face will surely fail. We will win our freedom because the sacred heritage of our nation and the eternal will of God are embodied in our echoing demands.[1]

King's words became reality. With his continued fight against discrimination in America, even after a bloody Sunday in Selma, Alabama, and even after the cost of his own life, his words and deeds rang true, and a new era began for millions of black Americans. Like General MacArthur, Martin Luther

King Jr. was a man with integrity. These men gave much of themselves to bring about the freedom of others, and in so doing followed the way of Christ.

* * * *

Remember the four chaplains at the beginning of the book? They had not been in the army very long before a torpedo sank their ship. They were perhaps proud to put on their uniforms for the first time; glad when fellow soldiers recognized them by their crosses or tablets and called them chaplain; proud to leave America and set sail for Europe on a quest to give freedom to others. In wearing the cross or the tablets and in believing they had a different destiny than the other men who served on the ship with them, they held to a distinct identity. They embodied the beliefs of soldiering even in crisis, past the point when most men were fleeing for self-preservation. Instead of seeking a lifeboat, the four chaplains instinctively believed they should help others and rescue as many soldiers as possible without regard for their own safety.

How do you see yourself? Do you embody a set of beliefs? Do you occupy a different destiny than the men who serve beside you? After taking the diagnostic, you have one view of yourself, that of either a Sentry, a Salesman, a Scout, or a Statesman. I would like to suggest that as each man patterns his life after Christ, the Master Statesman, he can become a Statesman as well. When Philip asked Jesus if He could show the disciples the Father, Jesus declared that to see Him in human flesh was to see the Father (John 14:8-9). The essence of the Father was in Jesus. In a similar way, when people meet a Christian man of integrity, in a sense, they have thus met Christ.

As Jesus is a sacrificial servant, so are we to be. As Jesus is a Statesman, so are we to be. But how do we get there?

To live the life of a Statesman, a man needs a plan—and not just any plan, but a *good* plan! Sometimes we men can let things ride awhile without adjusting the steering wheel. But it is important for every man to have a strategy and follow it.

So often, men will read a book like this and then set it down and continue with the status quo. We have good intentions for about seventy-two hours, and then it is right back to our old life habits. This chapter attempts to give two practical applications for what has been taught: first, forming and meeting with a small group of men; second, developing an individual improvement plan for specific aspects of your life. Any man who practices and applies these tools will make great progress toward living the life of a Statesman.

A Band of Brothers

Have you ever read in the book of Daniel about three Hebrew men who defied a king? They were bold and brash in their disobedience, yet God provided for them. What is striking to me is not only how they stood together when sentenced to death and thrown into a furnace but also the highly charged, politically incorrect words they delivered to the king.

King Nebuchadnezzer told them that if they did not

worship his golden image, they would be cast into a burning fiery furnace. Then he asked, "What god is there who can deliver you out of my hands?" (Daniel 3:15).

Their response:

> We do not need to give you an answer concerning
> this matter. If it be so, our God whom we serve is
> able to deliver us from the furnace of blazing fire;
> and He will deliver us out of your hand, O king. But
> even if He does not, let it be known to you, O king,
> that we are not going to serve your gods or worship
> the golden image that you have set up.
> DANIEL 3:16-18

What brass. Essentially, they told him to *step off*! And that God could definitely save them from the fire, but even if God chose not to, they would continue to serve Him rather than the king.

The king's response was typical. His pride was bruised, so in anger, he told the furnace workers to stoke the fire to seven times hotter than normal. Moments later, the king ordered that the three men be thrown inside the scorching flames. You are probably familiar with the rest of the story. The flames were so hot that the king's workers who threw the offenders into the furnace were burned to death, but the three Hebrew men were miraculously saved.

God honors those who honor Him (1 Samuel 2:30).

The apostles had a moment like this in Acts 4. The rulers

and scribes warned them to never speak or teach in the name of Jesus again. But as we learn, "Peter and John answered them, 'Whether it is right in the sight of God to listen to you rather than to God, you must judge, for we cannot but speak of what we have seen and heard'" (Acts 4:19-20, ESV).

What God-honoring brass. Essentially, they told them to *step off*! As in the story of the four chaplains, I cannot help but imagine that the courage and bravery of some of the stronger men helped the weaker men to stand firm and united. Some men can be singularly bold, but most of us are much more courageous when there is a man or two at our side.

One of the keys to living as a Statesman is to have other men in your life who can stand by your side to keep you brave and accountable. This book was designed to be read as part of a small group Bible study with other men. It is okay to read it by yourself, but going through the attached discussion guide with others will bring the message home, so to speak, and enable true opportunities for life change. Which men in your life do you like to spend time with and can you trust for deep conversations? Please consider reaching out to a few men right now to establish a connection.[2]

Make a Decision and Stick with It

I can be my own worst enemy when it comes to progress in the spiritual life. I have great intentions, but the follow-through is sometimes lacking. And then when I do follow through, I can struggle with consistency. For me, it is impor-tant to have an individual improvement plan. I follow four steps: acknowledge the situation, make a statement about it, find a solution to fix it, and then stick with the approach until I achieve victory. Four "S" words can be used with this model: Situation, Statement, Solution, and Steadfastness.

1. Decide what needs to be done (Situation)
2. State your intentions (Statement)
3. Follow up your words with actions (Solution)
4. Be consistent (Steadfastness)

For example, this is what it would look like with the specific situation of a man leading his family in devotions:

1. A man sees that his family is not connecting well, and he wants to have some spiritual input into their lives (Situation).
2. The man decides his family should have time together for Bible study and—after discussing this with his wife—explains to his family that they will meet for devotions every Thursday evening (Statement).
3. Each week, the family meets for Bible study and begins to pray for each other and care for each other (Solution).
4. When things come up and schedules change, the man reschedules his family's prayer time instead of canceling it (Steadfastness).

This is obviously not rocket science. But it happens to be where the battle is. It is very easy to watch television or go to the movies with your family. However, when we try to institute something of a spiritual nature in our families, it seems as if every force assails us, including sicknesses, out-of-town visitors, and special projects with short deadlines. As believers, we have declared ourselves on the battlefield. We should expect the stress and hardships of combat.

I am reminded here of Joshua. In speaking to the Israelites, he made a great declaration of strength: "Choose for yourselves today whom you will serve . . . but as for me and my house, we will serve the LORD" (Joshua 24:15). Joshua decided what needed to be done, he stated his intentions, and he gave an opportunity for other Israelites to join him—a declarative, bold act of leadership, wisdom, and strength. What is an area in your personal life that needs to be addressed?

1. What needs to be done? (Write it here.)

2. State your intentions.

3. Follow up your words with actions. For instance, if you wrote that tomorrow you will read your Bible for ten minutes before work, then, on the next day, *git 'er done.*

4. Be consistent.

*　*　*　*

I started the book discussing Roosevelt's speech entitled "Citizenship in a Republic." I would like to readdress it now.

It is not the critic who counts; not the man who points out how the strong man stumbles or where the doer of deeds could have done them better. The credit belongs to the man who is actually in the arena, whose face is marred by dust and sweat and blood.

What is it you need to do *now*? What in your life needs to change? Whenever we step out in faith, we become like the man in the arena. Whenever we take a moment to speak words of truth to our families, we are in the arena. Whenever we perform a deed for our church or employer, we are in the arena. When we decide to go the extra mile for a stranger or our neighbor, we are in the arena. When we decide whether to keep our word or not, we are standing in the doorway of the arena.

Always remember this: *When you are in the arena, you are not alone!* God is with you. As a Christian, you have His words available to you, words of honesty and honor. You also have His strength of character to empower your life. This power is a vast reservoir that, when tapped, is never lessened. Allow God to use your mouth, and allow Him to use your body to accomplish His will. Isaiah 49:2 states, "He has made My mouth like a sharp sword, in the shadow of His hand He has concealed Me; and He has also made Me a select arrow, He has hidden Me in His quiver."

We are God's sharp sword.

We are God's select arrow.

We are to be used as God's Statesmen.

Therefore, we are ambassadors for Christ, as though God were making an appeal through us.

2 CORINTHIANS 5:20

CHAPTER 10

THE DECISION

If you choose to join us I will be personally very grateful.

A LITTLE-KNOWN SPEECH given to a group of deserters during the American Civil War might have won the entire war for the Union Army. The speech was delivered by a former university professor, Joshua Lawrence Chamberlain, a colonel in the Twentieth Maine Regiment. In 1863, just before the Battle of Gettysburg, Colonel Chamberlain's unit was given an opportunity to plus up with 120 mutineers from another regiment. Chamberlain wanted these men to fight in his regiment, knowing that the rebels he would face were vicious warriors. However, he soon discovered that the 120 men were holding to a promise given to them at their initial enlistment that they would only have to serve two years, not three. They felt they were being unfairly treated by the Union

Army and wanted to be freed from their commitment. The Union Army held that since it was during war, they could be retained; if they did not fight, they would be shot.

Colonel Chamberlain spoke to the men and told them he agreed they were unfairly treated. He then fed them a meal and delivered a simple speech. Of the 120 mutineers, 114 agreed to join his regiment and fight. The following is part of his speech.

I've been ordered to take you men with me, I'm told that if you (laughs quietly) don't come I can shoot you. Well, you know I won't do that. Maybe somebody else will, but I won't, so that's that. Here's the situation, the whole Reb army is up that road aways waiting for us, so this is no time for an argument like this, I tell you. We could surely use you fellahs, we're now well below half strength. . . .

This regiment was formed last summer, in Maine.

There were a thousand of us then, there are less than 300 of us now. . . .

This is a different kind of army.

If you look back through history you will see men fighting for pay, for women, for some other kind of loot.

They fight for land, power, because a king leads them, or just because they like killing.

But we are here for something new, this has not happened much, in the history of the world.

We are an army out to set other men free.

America should be free ground, all of it, not divided by a line between slave states and free—all the way from here to the Pacific Ocean.

No man has to bow. No man born to royalty.

Here we judge you by what you do, not by who your father was.

Here you can be something.

Here is the place to build a home.

But it's not the land, there's always more land.

It's the idea that we all have value—you and me.

What we are fighting for, in the end, we're fighting for each other.

Sorry, I didn't mean to preach.

You go ahead and you talk for awhile.

If you choose to join us and you want your muskets back you can have them—nothing more will be said by anyone anywhere.

If you choose not to join us well then you can come along under guard and when this is all over I will do what I can to ensure you get a fair trial, but for now we're moving out.

Gentlemen, I think if we lose this fight we lose the war, so if you choose to join us I will be personally very grateful.[1]

One of the mutineers swayed to fight by Chamberlain's gracious words was Sergeant Andrew Tozier. He ended up carrying the Twentieth Maine flag as the color-bearer. As the conflict at Gettysburg progressed, the battle at Little Round Top was seen as one of the most decisive in all the war. On July 2, Chamberlain's troops held off the Confederate Army, who repeatedly tried to break the extreme left of the Union position. Tozier was often seen in the middle of the fight, raising the honor flag bravely, even though he had so recently been in custody as a deserter.

When all of their ammunition was depleted, Chamberlain issued his famous order for a bayonet charge, one last, desperate attempt to stop the rebels. It worked, and both he and Sergeant Tozier earned the Medal of Honor that day for conspicuous gallantry at the risk of life and above the call of duty.[2]

*   *   *   *

The mutineers that Chamberlain led were going to be tried for desertion and possibly die an ignominious death as deserters. Chamberlain spoke to them, believed in them, and gave them the opportunity to change direction and make something of themselves—to regain their integrity. All of us men have things in our past of which we are not proud. None of us have lived a perfect life. However, there are times when we are given a break, cut some slack, and extended an opportunity to excel. If we grab on to those chances, it is in those times we might feel most like men.

Usually, in that moment of opportunity, a decision has to be made, one that might alter your life forever. There might be fear associated with the decision because you could be afraid you will lose something that you once enjoyed or be humiliated in front of people you respect. Sergeant Tozier might have lost his life in the Battle of Gettysburg. Nonetheless, a decision had to be made.

There are many good examples in the Bible of men at crucial decision points: Jacob's decision regarding his brother, Esau; Samson's last, dying action while chained between two pillars; David's fear of King Saul; Rehoboam when confronted with a request from Israel's laborers; Daniel on whether to obey the edicts of the Medes and Persians; Joseph when confronted with Mary's unexpected pregnancy; Peter when asked by Jesus to give up his nets; the rich young ruler on whether to follow Jesus; Pilate when faced with the decision to release a prisoner; and Paul after his encounter with Christ.[3] Some made wise decisions and some did not. In every one of these men's lives, it seems, there was an opportunity to step out in faith and do something that reason might not suggest. Those who took steps of faith succeeded; those who hedged and played it safe ultimately failed.

In every man's life there is an opportunity for greatness. And it is usually connected with the man tapping into the fountain of God's love and truth. When a man uncovers that rare opportunity to step out in faith and live with integrity— no matter how foolish or dangerous it might seem—he must act on it or be rendered morally obsolete.

* * * *

There are many decision-making models in psychology today. The one we utilize in the military contains seven steps. It is based on the military method for problem solving and includes mission analysis and developing multiple courses of action.

At every army course I ever attended, my professors have beaten into my head the importance of identifying the problem before making a decision. The *most* important step before a decision is made, they taught me, is to clearly articulate the problem with all of its facts and assumptions, even if doing so takes the lion's share of your time.

Several quotes have been thrown around about having one hour to solve a problem. Some are even attributed to the genius Albert Einstein. The idea is usually stated in the following form: "If I had an hour to solve a problem and my life depended on determining the solution, I would spend the first fifty-five minutes defining the problem and the next five minutes solving it." This concept, which is compatible with my military training, is a counterintuitive proposition. Most people, when confronted with a problem, move immediately into problem-solving mode. However, there is much to be gained from closely considering the actual problem.

What is your problem today? What are the issues you are struggling with? What are the bad habits that you constantly feel the need to confess? Here is a list of some potential problem areas in your life:

- Addiction to prescription meds or other drugs
- Addiction to video games
- Adultery
- Fantasies/living a secretive life
- Flirting with a woman other than your wife
- Gambling
- Greed
- Indulgent drinking
- Laziness
- Neglecting family
- Overeating
- Racism
- Seeking vengeance
- Stealing from employer/government
- Suicidal thoughts
- Viewing pornography
- Withdrawal from family and others
- Workaholism
- Other (_____)

This is not a comprehensive list. In the small group portion of this book, the list will appear again, and you will be asked to indicate which of these issues you are currently struggling with. If you want, you can circle them now. Some men might be embarrassed to outwardly acknowledge one of their problems. What if someone else picked up your book and looked at it? The odds are, though, that with our perception gaps, some of the people in our lives already know about our struggles and are praying for us.

The evil in us is deeper than we can ever imagine. The issues on the list on the previous page are just manifestations of the immense human problem of sin. Those items are abnormal to the lives we know we are supposed to have, abnormal to the lives that God stands ready to give us power to live. We only solve our dilemma when we look to Christ and model that perfect, charitable life that He lived. He is the pattern to live by, hope for, and model to others. Only by living as Christ did can we partly gain—though sometimes unclearly—lives in the human experience of wholeness, freedom, and victory.

If you see your one big problem on the list above, the important thing for this chapter is to recognize it for what it is. Confess your problem, and ask for strength from God to be sustained without it. Decide to put that sin or struggle away from you, and move forward in faith, investing your time in the force multipliers and modeling the words of Jesus in the Sermon on the Mount. Many of us men know what we are supposed to do, but we consciously decide not to do it. Life seems easier when we let things ride, but there are long-term implications for procrastination. Not deciding to address a sin is a decision.

I have dealt with several of the areas listed above. They were indeed problems—sin areas in my life that needed a corrective. A better man should have written this book. But I believe it is our honesty, vulnerability, and transparent integrity that help lead us out of the pit. Shining light on our problems is the first step.

I wish I could deal with a problem area and then never have to face it again. In fact, I wish spiritual growth was easy. But, as a friend recently reminded me, a blade of grass only grows one day's length in one day's time.

*   *   *   *

Are you ready for life change? Are you ready to make a decision that will positively impact your life and the lives of those around you? Do you want to be a man of integrity? Do you want to be known by others as a man of character? The things we do and say echo in eternity. Life is short. Eternity is long. We hold in our hands a brief opportunity to make a difference in other people's lives.

The mutineers that Chamberlain led made a decision to fight, and that decision influenced the entire war. Chamberlain's decision to inspire rather than threaten them influenced their decision. And so on and so on. A decision for godliness will influence your entire life and the lives of those around you. Can you hear those words? *If you choose to join us I will be personally very grateful.*

The Statesman in you is calling out.

Do you have a stomach for this fight?

Are you ready to decide?

THE STRENGTH ALL MEN NEED

Chaplain, God found my radios!

IN THE CRUCIBLE OF WAR, you get the chance to see what men are really made of.

During a combat mission in Iraq, I worked with a commander who had a short fuse. Sometimes, he would yell and throw things around the room. On one occasion, I entered the room as he was frightening his subordinates. Everyone except the commander happily departed, leaving us alone. I asked him what he was so angry about.

The commander said, "I lost some radios, chaplain, and they're going to fry me for it."

"What do you mean?"

"I mean we just completed an inventory of the command equipment and we are missing four military radios.

And you know how the army works. They were not bought at Walmart, Chaplain. These radios cost thousands of dollars apiece, and I am going to be held responsible for them. My superior officer told me he was going to write a statement of charges against me if I did not find them soon."

I thought for a moment, then asked if I could pray for him to find the radios.

"You think that will help?" he asked, with a slight mock to his voice.

"It can't hurt."

"Sure enough, go ahead."

I prayed a simple prayer, short and sweet, and that was it. He went his way; I went my way. I soon forgot about the entire event. Two weeks later, the commander burst through the chapel doors looking for me. He had never set foot in the chapel during the entire deployment. "Chaplain," he exclaimed. "God found my radios!"

"What do you mean?" I asked.

"The radios were found by the military police, and they dropped them off at my office this morning."

The incident made the commander realize he needed to change his life, and he asked how to get started. I suggested meeting with me for a Bible study once a week. He agreed, and for the next few months I met with the commander on most Monday nights. We went through the Gospel of John together. It was fun for me to have someone ask all sorts of crazy questions I had never heard before, but that somehow seemed the point of it all. The Gospel seemed to be written for him. The commander developed faith, and I watched God shape a human heart.

More than a year later, after a period of reunion with my family in Minnesota, the army moved us to the East Coast. After our move, I was asked to preach at a small country church in rural New Jersey. As part of my sermon, I used the story of the commander to explain how God answers even the simplest of prayers.

After the service, a man approached me in the parking lot and inquired whether I had a moment. He asked me where I was, specifically, when I was with the commander. I told him. He asked what particular week, month, and year the radios were found. I told him. For a moment, I thought he was going to try to discredit my experience. He did just the opposite.

He had worked at the same forward operating base where I was stationed and during the same period, though we had never met in Iraq. The man was a government contractor and had been away from his family for a year, helping the war effort as a civilian. One day, while walking to the building where he worked, he happened to glance at a Dumpster and saw several shipping boxes in it. He investigated and discovered that the boxes housed brand-new army equipment—radios—that someone had thrown into the Dumpster. He picked them out of the trash, transported the boxes over to the military police, and turned them in.

Based on our calculation, this was at the same time and place that my commander's radios were found, which had freed him from an embarrassing and expensive ordeal.

God had moved me from Iraq back to Minnesota, then from Minnesota to New Jersey, and introduced me to the sole person He used to answer a prayer and change a man's life. Out of hundreds of millions of people in the United States, and tens of thousands of churches I could have been asked to preach at, God led me to the very church with the specific man in it who found the radios.

"Thank you," I told the contractor, after some words finally came to me.

"For what?" he asked.

"For being faithful and doing that good deed."

He could have kept the radios and sold them for a profit. He could have decided he did not have time to be bothered with the situation—like the priest and the Levite in the Good Samaritan parable. He could have been so distracted he did not even notice them. *Who looks in the garbage Dumpster?* However, this man did the right thing. He decided to do good that day, and a nonbeliever's life was changed as a result. This man had proved to be a man of integrity and honor.

"Aw, they were just a few radios," he said, smiling. "But I was pretty surprised when you told that story in church today."

I'll bet he was.

After I reflected on the event, I could clearly identify the undisputed hero of the story—God. I had said some words in prayer. That New Jersey contractor had performed a good deed. Words and deeds. These two items were the agents God used to reach the young commander. And, eighteen months later, God connected two of the three protagonists in a humble church on an old country road near a no-name town to give me a glimpse of what He does behind the scenes to change human history.

God was the force behind me, who offered to pray that the commander would find his radios.

God was the force behind the contractor, who found the radios and decided to do the right thing.

God was the force behind the young commander, who received his radios and then desired to be in a Bible study.

Everything we encounter in life somehow displays the magnificence of God—through His love, knowledge, or power. He is your strength, your shield, and your sustainer (Psalm 28:7 and 54:4). He will never fail you nor forsake you. He is the strength all men need. May we always remember that what matters most is not the measure of our strength but the *source* of our strength.

Before you close the cover of this book, will you pray the following prayer?

Lord, You are King over everything, including the smallest details of my life. Please help me to understand Your plan and purpose for my life and become a man who pleases You. May the words of my mouth and the deeds of my hands be acceptable in Your sight, O Lord. Please provide the wisdom and assurance I need every day to reach out to others in love, just as Christ showed me in His words and deeds as He walked on the earth. Your Word says I can do all things through Him who strengthens me. Please give me the strength to become a man of courageous integrity. In Jesus' name. Amen!

A ONE-SESSION DISCUSSION GUIDE FOR SMALL GROUPS

1. According to the author, what is a deed? What is a word? What is the definition of *integrity*? What is the distinction between ethics and morality? When the author writes that without alignment of words and deeds, "our lives will lack personal meaning and broader impact," what do you think he means?

2. Have you ever met a man who was all words and no deeds? What was he like? What about a man who was all deeds and no words? Have you ever met someone who had the perfect blend of both words and deeds? What was he like? What about a man with neither words nor deeds?

3. What profile did the diagnostic reveal you to be? Were your results a surprise? Why or why not?

4. After reading the introduction and the first chapter, do you believe that words and deeds have equal weight in the world? The author describes how deeds seem to be praised much more than words. Why is this so?

5. Briefly describe the difference between a Sentry, a Salesman, a Scout, and a Statesman. Are there more members of your group of friends with one profile over another? Why do you think that is?

6. In the introduction, the author mentions Martin Luther King Jr. and President Theodore Roosevelt as men mighty in both words and deeds. Can you think of other men who fit this bill?

7. What does it mean to be a man in the arena? Have you ever felt like you were there? Are you there now, or do you feel more like a spectator?

8. Why is it so hard for a man to keep his word?

9. The author discusses a moral code and how society has moved away from a common understanding of what it is. What has society replaced a moral code with? Is the replacement sustainable? What are the inherent dangers of *not* having a moral code?

10. What are the three adversity rules for the Statesman? Why do you think it would be helpful for a Statesman to remember these three things? Do you think it is easy to follow these rules? Why or why not?

11. The author identifies Jesus as the Master Statesman and attempts to prove his case. Is this case convincing? In the following chapter the author also appeals to all his readers to become Statesmen like Jesus. Do you think it is possible for *all* Christian men to achieve the level of Statesman? Or is it simply not attainable for some?

12. In chapter 7, the author gives seven examples of blind spots. If you are willing to share, are you now aware of possessing one or two of these blind spots?

13. What are the three integrity terrorists? Which one of the three do you think you find particularly challenging?

14. What is a force multiplier? What are the six force multipliers? Have you had any success in implementing a force multiplier on a regular basis? Please share about your experience with the group.

15. Is there one decision you have made to help improve your life as a result of reading this book? Would you be willing to share about this decision with the group?

16. In the final chapter of the book, the author states, "In every man's life there is an opportunity for greatness. And it is usually connected with the man tapping into the fountain of God's love and truth." Have you done this in your own life? Please explain.

A SIX-WEEK
BIBLE STUDY GUIDE
FOR SMALL GROUPS

Week 1 → The Authority of Christ (read the
introduction)

Week 2 → The Words of Christ (read chapters 1–2)

Week 3 → The Conduct of Christ (read chapters 3–5)

Week 4 → The Virtues of Christ (read chapter 6)

Week 5 → The Death and Resurrection of Christ (read
chapters 7–8)

Week 6 → The Call of Christ (read chapters 9–10)

The format for each week's study:

- Introduction and Reading Assignment
- Intel Brief
- Individual Journal Questions
- Prayer
- Small Group Questions
- Collective Thoughts

WEEK 1: THE AUTHORITY OF CHRIST

*Nearly all men can stand adversity, but if you want
to test a man's character, give him power.*

ABRAHAM LINCOLN

Both words and deeds matter in this life. Jesus was said to be
mighty in both (Luke 24:19). As a foundation for the next
five weeks, this week's focus is on the absolute authority of
Christ in all matters. This supremacy gives us assurance of
our faith and an example of how to treat others when placed
in positions of leadership. Only the Son of God could teach
with such authority.

Read:
- introduction, *Words and Deeds*
- the Gospel of Mark 1–3

INTEL BRIEF

At its essence, having authority means having power over
something. Authority can be given, it can be taken, and it
can be coerced. True authority means having true power or
complete control. It is from the Latin word *auctoritas*, which
means influence, prestige, warrant, or responsibility.

Jesus had an authority not given Him by heritage,
money, a ruling class, or a political entity. Jesus' power was
from within, wrapped in His personality and mission and
given from above. In one sense, He *was* authority, because

everything was made and held together through Him. The world had never seen power like this before.

All four Gospels contain an account of the life, ministry, and death of Jesus Christ, but the authority of Jesus is one of the Gospel of Mark's central themes. For instance, at the very beginning of Mark's Gospel, people are amazed at Jesus' teaching because it is with authority. Mark 1:27 states, "What is this? A new teaching with authority!" Mark also tells of Jesus' authority on earth to forgive sins. In Mark 2:1-12, Jesus speaks to a paralytic and tells him his sins are forgiven. The religious leaders take issue with this. Jesus challenges them by saying, "So that you may know that the Son of Man has authority on earth to forgive sins . . ." Then He forcefully—and fully—heals the man and tells him to go home. Not only did Jesus say He had authority, He showed everyone the proof of His authority.

Jesus had complete authority over one of the most sacred parts of Jewish theology: the Sabbath. In Mark 2, Jesus tells the Jewish leaders that He is Lord of the Sabbath—that He has power over it. He proves it by healing a man with a withered hand in a synagogue. Jesus also had authority over demons. Mark 1:34 says Jesus cast out many demons. Jesus' authority is seen in how He rebuked them, forbade them to speak, and demanded that they leave their hosts. Again, the fact that the demons fled is proof of Jesus' genuine dominion and power.

Jesus also had authority over the body, including disease and death. He healed the sick, gave sight to the blind, and provided hearing to the deaf. Jesus made legs and backs straight and brought several people back to life. This was raw power never seen before. Jesus forcefully commanded people to get up, to proceed home, to sin no more, and to follow Him. He had authority over His disciples and imparted power to them (Mark 3:13-19), and Jesus had command over nature and the laws of physics. Everything was under His divine authority.

INDIVIDUAL JOURNAL QUESTIONS

1. Think of a leader you once had who was not very effective. How did you respond?

2. Were you loyal despite their lack of influence? Did you discuss their leadership with them?

3. Now think of a time that you were in leadership. How did you use your authority—with force or as a servant? What is one thing you would do differently during that time?

4. Read Mark 11:27-33. The Jews were testing Jesus' authority. They were trying to set a trap for Him to fall into. However, by questioning them about John's baptism, Jesus turned the tables on them. Jesus did to the Jews what they were trying to do to Him. Jesus gave the perfect response. He was

never ruffled and never responded like He was
under pressure. What does this tell you about
His authority?

PRAYER

Lord, all authority in heaven and on earth rests in
You. There is nothing You do not notice, and there
is no event outside Your control. Help me to trust
You with every aspect of my life. Help me to come
to You for assistance and not try to go it alone.
May I stop relying on alternative strengths and
trust in Your strength. May the authority granted
me be used to glorify You and to advance Your
Kingdom. Help me see my rightful place in Your
eyes. Teach me humility, patience, and endurance.
Amen.

SMALL GROUP QUESTIONS

1. Open in prayer.

2. Discuss: Which leader has commanded the most
   authority in your life? Describe the experience,
   whether negative or positive.

3. Read the story of Martin and Bruce (from chapter 7)
   out loud.

4. Discuss: Describe a situation you've experienced that was similar to the story of Martin and Bruce. Which role did you play? What could Martin do to create a positive work environment? Why is it sometimes hard to see the big picture when you are in charge? Is it easier to be a manager or to be managed? What perception gaps did Martin have? What gaps did Bruce have?

5. Read Mark 2:1-12.

6. Discuss: What is the context of this passage? What are your observations? What is the true meaning of the passage? What is its application?

7. Discuss: Where does Jesus' authority come from? How much authority does He have? Did He operate with limits? Could He use His power for evil? Did Jesus ever hurt anyone? Look at verses 3-5. Do you have friends who are that persistent? How can you be a bridge to Christ for those you know that are still in darkness? How do you lead people around you to Jesus?

8. Review the introduction of *Words and Deeds*. Take a moment to describe to the group the bravest thing you have ever done.

9. Discuss: Share what you wrote down in the Individual Journal Questions section. (People should feel free to pass.)

10. Teamwork: How can each individual participating in this study help his small group accomplish the mission of humble leadership?

11. Cross-thought (if time allows): Read Matthew 28:18-20. What is the relevance of Jesus' words in verse 18 to the rest of the passage? What is the relevance to your own life? What kind of power can we expect to have from Christ today?

12. Close in prayer after asking if anyone else has something to share with the group about Jesus' authority or a personal leadership challenge.

COLLECTIVE THOUGHTS

The main idea here is twofold. First, we have an amazing Lord to follow and obey. Nothing escapes His control or is outside His power. Jesus commanded the crowds with His teaching and His works, and sometimes just His gaze. He commands our lives as well. Second, we are not to be too hung up on our own authority. Scripture contains much more material on service and humility than on leading and power. It is the way Jesus led that we are to follow. He employed His authority to serve and minister to people. He used His life not for self-gain but to uplift others. When we find ourselves in places of influence and responsibility, we need to consider why God has given us authority: to uplift ourselves, or to uplift others?

What is one thing you should keep practicing? What is one thing you need to change? What is one thing to pray for?

- One thing to keep doing: _____
- One thing to change: _____
- One thing to pray about: _____

WEEK 2: THE WORDS OF CHRIST

> *Christianity is the greatest intellectual system the mind of man has ever touched.*
>
> FRANCIS SCHAEFFER

All men tend toward being either too gracious or too truthful. We are constantly faced with the dilemma of being either loving or honest. Jesus, however, was never in a quandary. He broke the mold and is described by John as full of grace and truth (John 1:14). Jesus was always gracious and truthful to His followers.

Read:
- chapters 1–2, *Words and Deeds*
- the Gospel of Mark 4–7

INTEL BRIEF

A parable is a fictitious story used to illustrate one main point, usually a moral lesson. A parable forces its listeners to not only use their imaginations to understand the central characters and who they represent but also to interpret the story's underlying message and discern how to apply that truth to their own lives.

Mark 4 explains the parable of the sower and the seed. The central truth to this story is that as word of the Kingdom is sown, sometimes it bears fruit, and sometimes it does not. In Mark 4:11-12, when Jesus' disciples ask Him about the meaning of the parables, He tells them, "To you has been given the mystery of the kingdom of God, but those who are outside get everything in parables."

When Jesus explains the parables for His disciples, He unlocks the eternal truths associated with them. At the same time, Jesus explains that He is intentionally confounding those people who believe they already understand the Kingdom, thinking that it is something they can grab by force and work to their advantage.

Before Christ, the people of Israel's view of God was unique in many ways, but most importantly in how God revealed Himself. For Israel, God did not primarily reveal Himself through images or nature; God revealed Himself through specific actions in history. Canaanites would learn about Baal by looking outside to see if something was growing, because Baal was a god of fertility. Babylonians would pull out their telescopes, because their gods were astral bodies. But for the Israelites—how did they know what God is like? The answer for them was "See creation, read about the patriarchs, and hear the stories of Moses and David. Our God meets with us in history and reveals Himself there."

Then came Jesus, saying the most bizarre things, like "The time is fulfilled, and the kingdom of God is at hand; repent and believe in the gospel" (Mark 1:15). He declared publicly that He was the bread that came down from heaven, and that if any man was thirsty, he should come to Him and drink. Though they measured everything—including how many steps a man could walk on the Sabbath—the Jews did not have a grid for this. When they challenged Jesus about His age and He declared that before Abraham was born, He existed, they tried to immediately kill Him. They could not see the continuity between Jesus and the God who had revealed Himself to them in history—that the same God who spoke to Abraham and performed mighty deeds for Moses was in their presence again in the life of Christ.

In the parables, Jesus spoke of two classes of people: those who could accept a new proclamation of the Kingdom and come to salvation and those who were unwilling or unable to accept that this human was doing God's work.

INDIVIDUAL JOURNAL QUESTIONS

1. What is your favorite parable from the Gospels? Why? What do you like about it?

2. Read Mark 4:1-20. When I was a student minister at the University of Nebraska, I led a coed Bible study composed solely of nonbelievers. These were the cool kids and party animals, who lived for today without a care in the world. I took them to this passage and then discussed it a little bit. One of the girls earnestly asked, "Would you please teach us how to be good soil?" Think about your own life right now. Are you the good soil that Jesus talks about here? Or are desires for wealth, power, or material things sucking all the energy out of you until you have none left for the Kingdom? How are you investing your life right now?

3. In Mark 7:14-23, Jesus compares eating with unwashed hands with living a sinful life. Of these items—"evil thoughts, fornications, thefts, murders, adulteries, deeds of coveting and wickedness, as well as deceit, sensuality, envy, slander, pride, and foolishness"—which ones are you struggling with now?

PRAYER

Lord, Your Word says that Your disciples have been given the mystery of the Kingdom of God. Lord, help us to have ears within our ears to hear from You, and open our eyes within that we might see You for who You really are, in our tragedies and in our triumphs. And help me trust You when the world seems to be caving in around me. Please keep me humble, knowing that You are the Lord, and You will not share Your glory with another. But help me also to experience Your love. I give Jesus the freedom to search out every area of my life and to change whatever He desires. May He be my Lord my entire life. Amen.

SMALL GROUP QUESTIONS

1. Open in prayer.

2. Discuss: In chapter 2, there is a definition of integrity and an explanation of ethics and morality. In your own words, what does it mean to have ethics? What does it mean to have morality? After explaining the difference between the two, discuss what it means when these concepts are in synthesis with each other.

3. Read the last paragraph in the Intel Brief section. Think of a time when you were scratching your head and wondering what God was doing with your life.

4. Discuss: When was a time when you were challenged regarding whether to take God at His word or not? Perhaps you have never been

seriously tested in life and things have moved along swimmingly. Have you learned about God from others' trials?

5. Read Mark 4:1-20.

6. Discuss: What is the context? What are your observations? What is the true meaning of the passage? What is its application?

7. Discuss: On first glance, the story—along with Jesus' explanation—makes fairly good sense. What is a modern-day example of the first soil (road)? What is a modern-day example of the second soil (rocky ground)? How are these first two soils different? What is a modern-day example of the third soil (thorns)? What is a modern-day example of the fourth soil (good soil)? Who is someone that you can see is being good soil for the Lord? Now for the hard part: In verses 11-12, Jesus speaks of those people who are never allowed to understand. Without going into a debate over God's sovereignty versus free will, is it explained in Scripture why Jesus used parables and kept some people from understanding the truth of His mission? Why the secrecy? Shouldn't everyone have the full knowledge of God? Matthew 13:10-17 might help with these last questions.

8. Pre-work: Ask if anyone would like to share some of the items they wrote down for questions 1–3 in the Individual Journal Questions section.

9. Teamwork: How can each individual participating in this study help the small group accomplish the mission of being good soil at work, at home, at church, and with friends?

10. Cross-thought (if time allows): Read Matthew 13:24-30. Why does the landowner allow the tares to grow? Does this make sense? Read Matthew 13:36-43. Wouldn't it be easier just to have wheat in the field? Or is this all part of some great test?

11. Close in prayer after asking if anyone else has something to share with the group.

COLLECTIVE THOUGHTS

The Judaism of first-century Palestine believed that God's rule would come eventually—at the end of history. It was understood that if you obeyed Moses' teachings and lived a good life, you would be rewarded when God brought the world to an end. Jesus taught something radical in the parables, and it confused His listeners. Jesus was saying that God already ruled; in the person of Jesus, God's Kingdom was inaugurated. Jesus taught His disciples that His rule in the present was quiet and simple and could only be discerned through eyes of faith. It was not recognizable to the world or acknowledged by the world—only perceived through eyes of faith. God's rule and reign was present, even under the domination of the Romans.

With Christ's explanation of the soils, He showed that many things could rob His word from the hearts of men. However, those who truly listened to Him and obeyed His teachings would accomplish much in this lifetime, including gaining eternal life. The Jews were looking for a different kind of savior, one who would bring them victory over their tormentors. Jesus was teaching that their deliverer was already among them. With the parable of the mustard seed in Mark 4:30-32, Jesus taught that the Kingdom of God—though visibly small like a seed—was there in the present and would quickly become the most important thing in life. He was teaching that through Christ, God was establishing His Kingdom, and that eventually, it would reign supremely over all He created.

WEEK 3: THE CONDUCT OF CHRIST

The real test of a saint is not one's willingness
to preach the gospel, but one's willingness to do
something like washing the disciples' feet.

OSWALD CHAMBERS

Christ did not come as a conquering king but as a suffering servant. He refused to allow anyone or anything to make Him into something He was not. His identity and mission as Messiah was not what the Jews expected but what they desperately needed: a servant. We, too, can serve when we do so from an overflowing heart.

Read:

- chapters 3–5, *Words and Deeds*
- the Gospel of Mark 8–10

INTEL BRIEF

For some reason, Jesus wanted many of His great deeds to go unnoticed by the masses. He refused to let others spread the good word about His healings. This is evidence of what theologians call the "Messianic Secret."[1] Jesus knew His identity as the long-awaited Messiah but did not want the crowds or the Jews to know who He was until the time of His death. The Gospel of Mark highlights this aspect of Jesus' ministry more fully than any other Gospel.

Early on, when Jesus began to reveal His unusual power, He ordered those around Him to be silent. When Jesus healed a man with leprosy (Mark 1:40-42), He commanded him not to tell anyone about it. However, the man went out and spoke freely about it, to such a degree that Jesus could not go anywhere openly because of the crowds seeking after Him. In Mark 5, Jesus brings a synagogue official's daughter back to life. After the little girl arises and begins to walk, Jesus gives the parents strict orders that no one should know about what happened (verse 43). In Mark 7:32-37, Jesus heals a man who is deaf and dumb, then immediately tells those watching not to tell anyone about it. Yet Mark writes that the more Jesus ordered people to be quiet, the more widely they would proclaim His power.

Jesus also told the demons to be quiet. In Mark 1:25, Jesus commands an unclean spirit who calls Jesus "the Holy One of God" not to speak. In Mark 1:34, Jesus does not allow the demons to speak because they know who He is. In Mark 3:11-12, when Jesus casts out unclean spirits and they behold Him, they declare Jesus the Son of God. Jesus then warns them not to make Him known.

Jesus even instructed the disciples not to make known to others who He was. In Mark 8:30, after Peter declares that Jesus is the Christ, Jesus warns the disciples to tell no one about Him. Similarly, immediately after the transfiguration, Jesus told His companions not to tell anyone what they had seen until after His resurrection.

Why all the secrecy? Didn't Jesus *want* people to understand who He was? One good reason for this silence was that Jesus' ministry might have ended quickly if the Jewish leaders and Romans heard that a prospective Messiah was in the area. The first century was a tumultuous era; insurrection was a popular proposal in Jesus' day. If Jesus had allowed this belief to take root, He would not have had much time to heal people or teach His disciples.

Jesus ordering the demons to silence makes perfect sense, knowing who Jesus really was. He did not want agents of the adversary—who were known for their lies—to be His heralds. But the most important reason for Jesus' commands for silence must be that His mission hinged on something deeper than anyone could have known at the time. Instead of a Messiah as a political leader, Jesus came as a Messiah who would serve and suffer, a Messiah more recognizable in the servant hymns of Isaiah than in the mighty warrior themes from the Psalms. The crowds were expecting someone to free them. Jesus would bring freedom, but not in the way they expected. The people's problem was not Rome—it was their own sin and the adversary. The essence of sin is selfishness, and the values of the Kingdom Jesus inaugurated are summarized in the word *selfless*. Jesus was not self-seeking; He came to serve.

It was right that people wanted to go out and tell others what Jesus had done for them. When Christ touches your life, you cannot keep quiet. However, Jesus' mission was more than displaying God's power: It was an emptying, and it was taking on the form of a servant. This service would end in the ultimate sacrifice, and no one could see that end but Christ alone, so He called for secrecy.

INDIVIDUAL JOURNAL QUESTIONS

1. Think of a time when someone truly served you. How did it make you feel? How did you respond to them during the event and afterward? Think of one person you can serve this week and write their name below. Now, think of a specific way you can serve them and write this next to their name. Ask God to give you the strength to follow through.

2. After reading through chapter 5 of *Words and Deeds*, you have identified from the diagnostic which profile you are: Sentry, Salesman, Scout, or Statesman. How well do you identify with what the author has proposed for your type? Do the R, S, T, and L categories (page 40) apply to you? Why or why not?

3. In Mark 8:27-34, Jesus has an intimate moment with His disciples, asking them who they think He is. Peter's response is absolutely correct, yet Christ tells the disciples to tell no one. Why was He so secretive about His identity? When Peter rebukes Jesus for mentioning His upcoming death, Jesus in turn rebukes Peter, calling him Satan. Have you ever been chastised for doing the right thing? Was Peter doing the right thing here? Could he have known the importance of Jesus' true mission at the time? At that point, could he have known Jesus' true identity as a suffering servant?

PRAYER

Lord, You came to earth clothed in humility, with a mission to serve others and suffer. Help me to be more like You. Please kill my pride and humble me, that I may see who I really am in Your eyes. Help me to have a deep love for other people and to have a sacrificial heart to serve them. Help me not to get bitter and frustrated when I think I am being taken advantage of. Help me to trust You in all situations and know that You are the one I should aim to please. Amen.

SMALL GROUP QUESTIONS

1. Open in prayer.

2. Discuss: Of the leaders you've worked for, which one has displayed the most humility and service to others? Describe the experience and what you learned by working alongside this individual.

3. Read each of the four profiles in chapters 4 and 5: Sentry, Salesman, Scout, and Statesman (if not done already).

4. Discuss: Which one of the four types of men are you? Do you agree with this assessment? Why or why not?

5. Read Mark 5:21-24 and 35-43.

6. Discuss: What is the context? What are your observations? What is the true meaning of the passage? What is its application?

7. Discuss: Where does Jesus' power to heal come from? How much power does He have? Are there any limits? Notice how quickly the people in the house change their emotions between verse 38 and verse 40. Why does the crowd laugh at Him? In verse 43, Jesus gives them strict orders that no one should know about this. Why does He do this? What is the significance that Jesus, during His life, raised people from the dead?

8. Review: Now that you are familiar with the four types of men, look again at the story of Martin and Bruce from chapter 7. In this story, try to identify the Statesman, the Scout, the Salesman, and the Sentry. Also, if time allows, think of the main disciples. Who were the Statesmen, Scouts, Salesmen, and Sentries? Think of those you currently work with. Do most people you know fit into one of these categories?

9. Pre-work: Ask if anyone would like to share some of the items they wrote down for questions 1–3 in the Individual Journal Questions section.

10. Teamwork: How can each individual participating in this study help his "team" accomplish the mission of a servant heart?

11. Cross-thought (if time allows): Read Luke 17:7-10. What is the meaning of Jesus' words in verse 9? How does it relate to His own mission?

12. Close in prayer after asking if anyone else has something to share with the group about Jesus' identity as a sacrificial servant.

COLLECTIVE THOUGHTS

The main idea here has to do with Jesus' identity as a suffering servant. Isaiah 53 describes the Messiah as a man of sorrows acquainted with grief. It also states He is oppressed and afflicted, and He is called "My Servant." Often, we look to God for help to make us someone important or to accomplish something great. Jesus as a suffering servant teaches us something about the hidden things of God. Christ was born in a Bethlehem stable to commoners, not in Rome to a prince and princess. Yet He was still victorious over sin and death. His victory can even be seen in our brokenness and struggles in this life. When we give our lives fully to Him, He can straighten our paths with His wisdom and provide roses from our ruins.

What is one thing you should keep practicing? What is one thing you need to change? What is one thing to pray for?

- One thing to keep doing: _____
- One thing to change: _____
- One thing to pray about: _____

WEEK 4: THE VIRTUES OF CHRIST

*Courage is not merely one of the virtues but the
form of every virtue at the testing point.*

C. S. LEWIS

Chapter 6 looks at the virtuous life of Christ. Jesus was
the model of integrity when He walked on earth as the
Master Statesman. His life teaches us about love, compassion, generosity, humility, hope, and many other character
traits. We can study the life of Christ and learn from His
example.

Read:

- chapter 6, *Words and Deeds*
- the Gospel of Mark 11–12

INTEL BRIEF

The virtues Jesus teaches us do not come in a list. Jesus
teaches us virtues by how He lived His life. Jesus shows us
how to be pure in an evil world, and He instructs us to keep
God at the center of all our encounters, especially when we
are tempted. Jesus showed love to His disciples and to those
He ministered to by healing them, teaching them, and caring
for them. Jesus showed compassion to the multitude by feeding them. In this feeding, we see His generosity when a total
of nineteen baskets of food were left over. Jesus teaches us the
bounty of God here. He does not just give to His followers;

He gives abundantly. This abundance, Christ purported, would come of His disciples when the seeds of His words were sown in good soil to produce a crop of a hundredfold.

Jesus' life teaches us humility when He allowed Himself to be baptized, over the protests of John the Baptist. Jesus rode into Jerusalem on a donkey, when He rightfully could have come in on a horse with an army. Jesus, the King of the ages, washed His disciples' feet and taught them about humility and service. Jesus died naked (or nearly naked), listening to the rebukes of mockers.

Jesus' life teaches us about hope: He was constantly aware of His future death but preached about a new life with the Father. He spoke of His betrayal but was more concerned about the fate of the betrayer than about dwelling on the pain of being betrayed. Jesus' life teaches us about having faith: He told the disciples they just needed the tiniest amount of faith to allow God to work on their behalf—the faith of a mustard seed. He used faith to heal the deaf and blind, knowing His prayers would be answered. He used faith to consecrate the bread and the fishes for the masses, along with the bread and the wine for the disciples.

Jesus' life teaches us to live lives of courage, of patience, of goodness. He endured a tremendous fast in the desert and then allowed Himself to be tempted. He was patient with teaching the disciples important life lessons over and over again. His courage, patience, and goodness are examples to Christians and non-Christians alike in how to deal with adversity. When enemies tried to twist His words and His actions, Jesus responded not in anger or violence but in truth and grace, often showing them that the way God looked at something was entirely different from a human point of view.

Jesus teaches us about justice and restraint. He forbade His disciples from hindering people who were casting out demons in Jesus' name but not following Him. Christ told them that "those who are not against us are for us." He spoke to His disciples about the end of time, when God would punish the wicked. He forbade His disciples from exacting revenge (Luke 9:51-56). In all these things, Jesus is teaching His followers that God's plans are larger than the players, and that we should trust in His timing.

Jesus teaches us about holiness and sanctity in marriage. When the Jews asked Him about Moses' law to give a certificate of divorce, Jesus taught about the heart of God as purity, unity, and fidelity. "And they shall become one flesh," Jesus quoted from Genesis 2:24, and thus affirmed God's ancient principle of oneness as above the Old Testament law. The virtues Jesus teaches us are boundless. He was the model of integrity and a true Statesman.

INDIVIDUAL JOURNAL QUESTIONS

1. Who is the most virtuous man you know? What is it about that person that is the most important, or what draws you to him the most? Do you model his behavior sometimes or think about what response

he might have to a certain trial you might be
going through? How does this person remind you
of Christ?

2. In Mark 9:38-43, Jesus teaches His disciples about
restraint and how to get along with people who
do not work alongside them well. In your own
words, write out what Jesus is telling the disciples
in verses 39-40. Have you ever had to have
patience with someone in the ministry who saw
things completely differently than you? Were you
able to exercise restraint, or did your impatience
with them cause you some trouble? How did you
resolve the issue?

PRAYER

Lord, You lived the most virtuous life anyone could
have lived, and Your life is a model for all Christians.
Help me to reflect the glory of God in my daily life
by living a life of love and faith—like Christ. Help
me to be kind and generous to those in need. Please
give me wisdom and courage for the trials ahead and
hope that I might lead my family. In Your grace, You
have shown us a model life, a life that was pleasing to
God. Help me to be like You, in all my ways. Amen.

SMALL GROUP QUESTIONS

1. Open in prayer.

2. Discuss: What do you think of the C. S. Lewis quote at the beginning of this lesson? Does it make sense? Between what happens to us and our response is a space. In that space, we have the power to consider how to respond. With that in mind, why is it so hard to live a virtuous life sometimes? Can't we just *choose* to do what's right? Also, is it possible to live a life of virtue—like Christ, but two thousand years later?

3. Read the story of the two roofers at the end of chapter 2.

4. Discuss: Have you encountered businessmen like the first roofer? What did you do about it? One would think that roofers with integrity would have much more business than their less-ethical counterparts. Why aren't most companies operated with a high level of integrity? Or do you think they are? Why?

5. Read Mark 10:1-12.

6. Discuss: What is the context? What are your observations? What is the true meaning of the passage? What is its application?

7. Jesus taught His followers to live truly virtuous lives, many times turning a human precept upside down. Christ taught what God the Father thought about certain things, like having ceremonially clean hands as compared to a dirty heart (Mark 7:14-23). This passage seems to suggest that marriage is the crucible for living a virtuous life. To be married and have children strips the pride and selfishness out of a person pretty quick; otherwise, things go downhill fast. Why is it so hard to be a virtuous person in marriage? Does Jesus give us any option but to work issues out and change our behaviors with each other? How might the virtues of Christ presented in the Intel Brief section of this chapter help in married life? Is it possible to be a man of integrity, humility, and love in the workplace, at church, or with friends without those virtues taking place at home? Basically, can people fake it? Why would they want to? Have you been faking it in one or two of these areas?

8. Pre-work: Ask if anyone would like to share some of the items they wrote down for questions 1–2 in the Individual Journal Questions section. Has anyone

in the group had someone else take the Words and Deeds Diagnostic? If so, please explain if there were similar results or if they were different.

9. Teamwork: How can each individual participating in this study help his "team" accomplish the mission of being a virtuous person at work, at home, at church, and with friends?

10. Cross-thought (if time allows): Read Matthew 5:7-9. How does a man show mercy at work, home, and church today? Have you been used as a peacemaker at one of these areas? Define "pure in heart." Try to explain it in your own words.

11. Close in prayer after asking if anyone else has something to share with the group.

COLLECTIVE THOUGHTS

Christ's life was lived as an example for the ages. We do not have the same abilities and personality Christ had, but He expects His followers to exhibit moral excellence and to live virtuous lives. Consider ways that you might grow in the areas covered in this study. Ask a good friend to hold you accountable and to pray for you. Sometimes our friends can see when we are "faking it" faster than we can. One goal of this study is to challenge you to live without duplicity.

WEEK 5: THE DEATH AND RESURRECTION OF CHRIST

> *The love of God is greater far*
> *Than tongue or pen can ever tell;*
> *It goes beyond the highest star,*
> *And reaches to the lowest hell.*

FREDERICK M. LEHMAN

The death and resurrection of Jesus Christ are the most important events in human history; they place God's love on display. By these acts, Satan's power over men is destroyed, and humankind is brought the blessings of God's reign.

Read:
- chapters 7–8, *Words and Deeds*
- the Gospel of Mark 13–16

INTEL BRIEF

The death and resurrection of Christ is a twist—simultaneously the most evil and wonderful thing in the world. By the latter, humankind is afforded eternal life; by the former, the One who gives us eternal life is killed. Jesus' death and resurrection prove that He is the Son of God and that everything He taught was true. In his work *The Case for Christ*, Lee Strobel provides excellent research material for people to consider the evidence regarding the resurrection of Jesus Christ. For the purposes of this men's study, it is critical to consider the changed lives of the disciples and of the community of faith Jesus belonged to in the first century.

Scripture tells us the disciples were dispersed after Jesus was arrested. Peter denied Christ, and most of the others hid in fear. Not all of them attended the Crucifixion. Only two of them ran to the tomb to see if it was indeed empty. We see them back at their old career of fishing when Jesus encountered them on the beach. Some of them were walking in the country. And there is a sense in the Gospels that, for the most part, the disciples kept a low profile, scared of the Jewish rulers who had won round one in their battle against Christianity—or so it seemed.

In fact, even though Jesus told His disciples over and over again that He—the Messiah—would suffer but come back to life (Mark 14:27-28), they refused to believe Him. In Mark 16, Mary Magdalene went to where they were hiding to tell them that she saw Jesus alive, but they refused to believe her (verses 9-11). Two of them reported that they saw Him on the road, but the disciples did not believe them either (verses 12-13). Thomas did not even believe his fellow disciples when they said Jesus had visited them! These men were not prepared—emotionally or spiritually—for these encounters. In Mark 16:14, Jesus reproaches the disciples for their lack of belief in trustworthy eyewitnesses.

What we see next with the disciples, therefore, is important. These men invested their entire lives to preach to others that Jesus came back from the dead and ascended into heaven. There was nothing for them to gain from this except persecution. They themselves would know if Jesus' resurrection was true or not. Who would die for a lie? The only answer could be that these men had actually been with the resurrected Christ—in the flesh—eating with Him, talking to Him, praying with Him, and relating to Him again as a fully human, touchable person. These encounters changed the disciples' lives and the lives of many other followers as well. In one passage, it states Jesus was seen by more than five hundred people. This could explain the incredible beginning of the church in Jerusalem, the entrenched headquarters of Judaism for hundreds of years: Thousands of Jews converted and became Christians in the weeks following Jesus' resurrection.

Obviously, many religious founders are deeply admired by their adherents. But when you look at the life of Christ and consider the subjects taught in this Bible study—His miracles, His parables, His wisdom, His teaching, His servanthood—and wrap all of this together with His death and resurrection in order to save people from their sins, there is no close comparison between Christianity and any other religion.

If Christianity is true, then no other religion can be true, because Christ made such exclusive claims about Himself: "I am the way, and the truth, and the life; no one comes to the Father but through Me" (John 14:6). "I am the resurrection and the life; he who believes in Me will live even if he dies" (John 11:25). The disciples and those who were with them would know if Christian claims of a resurrection were true or not, and their lives preach to us that Jesus was indeed raised from the dead. They did not simply possess a blind or emotional faith from what others had told them. They held to a real encounter involving all of their senses over a period of time (1 John 1:1-3).

Consider also the lives of Jesus skeptics, like Saul of Tarsus, who encountered the risen Christ and had nothing to gain from his conversion but mockery and rejection from a hierarchical establishment that had groomed him to be a leader of leaders. Saul—renamed Paul after his conversion—put this career away, gave up everything, and followed Christ. There can be no other explanation except that the God of the Bible is the one true God, and the Jesus that Mark writes about is the only way to come to Him.

INDIVIDUAL JOURNAL QUESTIONS

1. Read Mark 15:22-39. Does it appear strange that so many people were there by Jesus' cross insulting Him? Write below something about this passage that you had not considered before.

2. The Intel Brief discusses the changed lives of the disciples after the resurrection of Jesus. Does the author make a convincing case for the resurrection? Or does it still seem like it cannot be proved by the actions of a few men? What do you think?

3. Some people struggle with the exclusivity of Christianity; they think that it seems too narrow. Could there be more than one way to God and to heaven? Consider the discussion in the Intel Brief about other religions not being true if Christianity is true. Do you agree with this assertion? If not, read John 11:25-27 and John 14:6. How do they measure up to the statements in the Intel Brief?

4. Chapter 7 of *Words and Deeds* discusses gaps. How large is your primary gap? Have you asked others to take the diagnostic for you? If so, what was the result of your perception gap? Were you surprised at how others viewed your words and deeds? Why or why not?

5. Rate yourself in the following seven areas. Circle the number on each line that corresponds with your answer. Then be prepared to talk about your responses with your group.

PRESENT CHARACTER LEVEL	POOR/ LOW				GREAT/ HIGH
Leadership	1	2	3	4	5
Servanthood	1	2	3	4	5
Boldness/Courage	1	2	3	4	5
Forgiveness	1	2	3	4	5
Humility	1	2	3	4	5
Honesty/Truthfulness	1	2	3	4	5
Kindness	1	2	3	4	5

PRAYER

Lord, Your Word declares that Jesus died a hideous
death, was buried, and then rose again to physical
life and was seen by hundreds of people. Help me
to believe this in the core of who I am. And help
me to be comforted knowing that Your Word is true
and that I can count on Christ as my Savior. Help
me to be bold like the disciples when I am given an
opportunity to share my faith. Remind me often that
You are King, that in Your Kingdom there are no
mistakes, and that everything that happens in my life
happens for a reason—and for my ultimate good—
because You love me. Amen.

SMALL GROUP QUESTIONS

1. Open in prayer.

2. Discuss: Who is the boldest person you have ever met? Is there a difference between boldness and courage?

3. Read the opening story of chapter 1, the story about the four chaplains.

4. Discuss: Have you ever had an intense encounter with a group of people that became lifelong friends as a result of their shared experience? How do you think those chaplains had the strength to stand and sing as the ship went down? Is it possible to *train yourself* to be ready for this type of traumatic encounter? Do you think there was a soldier in the oily water that night wishing he had stood alongside the four chaplains to allow another serviceman to have his life preserver?

5. Read Mark 16:1-14.

6. Discuss: What is the context? What are your observations? What is the true meaning of the passage? What is its application?

7. Discuss: The resurrection story is one of the most well-known stories in the Bible. From our perspective today, it seems crazy that it took so long for the disciples to believe that Jesus was alive. Jesus thought so too. This was another example of Jesus having to reproach His disciples for their hardness of heart. What were the reasons for their fear? What were the reasons for their lack of belief in the Jesus sightings? Transition to your own life. Have you ever had this kind of fear about being a Christian or being "found out" by someone at work or in the community? Have you ever refused to see Jesus in an event in your life? Or refused to believe in a miracle someone told you about? What is the difference between your story and that of the disciples?

8. Pre-work: Ask if anyone would like to share some of their insights or answers to questions 1–4 in the Individual Journal Questions section. Does everyone in the group understand the difference between a primary gap and a perception gap?

9. Teamwork: How can each individual participating in this study help his "team" accomplish the mission of being bold ambassadors of Jesus Christ's resurrection?

10. Cross-thought (if time allows): Read John 21:1-14. Why do you think Jesus gave His disciples this one last miracle with the fish? Why did Peter throw himself in the sea while the others rowed to shore? Why do you think Jesus had breakfast waiting for them? Any other observations about this passage that are striking?

11. Close in prayer after asking if anyone else has something to share with the group.

COLLECTIVE THOUGHTS

After three years together, the emotional connection the disciples shared after Jesus' death was strong. But the connection they shared after His resurrection was impenetrable. They would never go back and be the men they used to be. Peter, Andrew, Philip, Bartholomew, Simon, and James, son of Alphaeus, were all crucified. James and Matthew were killed with a sword. Thomas was killed by a spear, and Thaddaeus was killed by arrows.[2] These were just the disciples. Other followers were burned at the stake, thrown off cliffs, killed by large stones, sawn in half, or drowned for their faith. What is truly remarkable is that the followers of Christ became as bold as lions and decided to preach in the open square inside hostile Jerusalem. How has your life changed as a result of meeting Christ?

WEEK 6: THE CALL OF CHRIST

If Jesus Christ be God and died for me, then no
sacrifice can be too great for me to make for Him.

C. T. STUDD

Christ came to give us freedom. Peter and Andrew did not just leave their nets; they were made free from them. They found in Jesus a man who was worthy of all their time and energy. Though they struggled with their belief and their own pride, the disciples were "all in."

Read:

· chapters 9–10, *Words and Deeds*

INTEL BRIEF

The call that Jesus gave to His disciples is similar to the call that Jesus gives to men and women today. When they were called in first-century Palestine, the Twelve left their professions and families to begin a journey with Christ. In a similar way, Jesus calls men and women today to follow Him and trust Him with their lives. Essentially, Jesus is asking His followers to trade in their old nets—their old ways of perceiving the world and relating to others (and possibly even their professions). He also wants His followers to be influenced by what God wants them to do and how God wants them to relate. It starts with simple belief and proceeds into being transformed by Christ's challenges for us, as recorded in Scripture.

The initial call upon a life is that of salvation, to believe that Christ was not just an example to me but my substitute as atonement for my sins. Christ's death became my death, and His life became my life. It is through Jesus Christ that I have grace and am now free from God's condemnation. It is through Christ's blood sacrifice that I have been reconciled to God and have peace, so I will not experience God's wrath on Judgment Day. Also, it is through Christ's resurrection and life that I enter into eternal life. Because of Christ's life, I will have a full and future salvation and be restored to God eternally.

The Gospel of Mark shows that Jesus did not ask everyone He met into a discipleship relationship. And not everyone that Jesus called followed Him. In Mark 5, Jesus tells a man who wants to follow Him to go back home (verses 18-20). In Mark 10:17-22, Jesus invites a rich young ruler to follow Him, but the man walks away grieved, unwilling to part with his wealth.

What we find in Mark's Gospel is a theme not only of discipleship but also of discipleship failure. In the process of coming to terms with who Jesus was, the Twelve said and did some very vain things and displayed a lack of faith. For instance, in Mark 4, the disciples show a conspicuous lack of faith during a storm before Jesus stills the sea (verses 37-41). There was a lack of belief before Jesus fed the thousands. Peter misstepped when he rebuked Jesus, and in Mark 9, the disciples have their own conversation while Jesus discusses His upcoming death (verses 31-34). When He asks about their discussion, it is revealed they were debating which one of them would be the greatest.

These failures and vanities serve a great purpose for the reader, however, because it is here that we can glean how Jesus might respond to us when we also encounter failures of faith. In Mark chapter 9, Jesus tells the disciples that whoever wishes to be great must be a servant to all. Whoever wishes to be first, must be last. We also find Peter's triple denial of Christ and his redemption after the resurrection. These episodes of instruction and restoration can give great comfort and strength to those of us journeying today.

INDIVIDUAL JOURNAL QUESTIONS

1. Think of how you were first introduced to Christianity. Was it by your family, a friend, a church, or another ministry? Describe some of your first thoughts about what you observed about Christians. Did it attract you; was it repulsive? What is an event that sticks out in your mind when you changed your perception or actions?

2. Read Mark 1:16-20. Once, while I was leading a Bible study of international students, they were

indignant about the disciples' actions. "No one would leave their profession and their expensive nets to follow a man they just met," they said—"it is ridiculous!" I had never thought much about the passage before their protest, but I can see their point. What do *you* think about this account? Write down several key words or themes you notice in this passage. What questions does it raise for you? Why do you think the men left everything to follow Christ? Do you have a similar story?

3. In Mark 9:35, Jesus instructs His disciples a little bit about what it takes to be "all in." What He is describing to them is radical discipleship. It takes a power outside us to love an enemy, to forgive spouses who have wounded us, or to serve people who do not appreciate us. Radical discipleship is more than just a flash in the pan; it is a call to deep, long, intentional relationships. Who in your life needs you to love them unconditionally? Jesus demonstrated radical discipleship by walking alongside people where they were—who in your life needs you to walk alongside them? Radical discipleship also requires vulnerability—what is your high-risk area? In which life area do you need accountability?

4. Please circle the issue(s) you are currently dealing with:

- Addiction to prescription meds or other drugs
- Addiction to video games
- Adultery
- Fantasies/living a secretive life
- Flirting with a woman other than your wife
- Gambling
- Greed
- Indulgent drinking
- Laziness
- Neglecting family
- Overeating
- Racism
- Seeking vengeance
- Stealing from employer/government
- Suicidal thoughts
- Viewing pornography
- Withdrawal from family and others
- Workaholism
- Other (_____)

How long have you had these problems? What have you tried to do about it? Have you ever confessed these issues to a close friend or mentor? If you are married, have you shared them with your spouse? Please prayerfully consider opening up about these issues with your small group the next time you meet. Sharing a burden with another man is a helpful tool to climb out of the rut you might be in. "Iron sharpens iron, so one man sharpens another" (Proverbs 27:17).

PRAYER

Lord, You came so that I might enter into a relationship with You. Thank You for forgiving me my sins and offering me eternal life through the death and resurrected life of Jesus. I ask You to take complete control of my life and to make me the man You want me to be. I am tired of serving myself and I long to be led by You, learn how to live in grace, and learn how to live an other-oriented life. Open me up to Your ways, give me the strength to follow Your leadership, and help me to help others in this journey. Amen.

SMALL GROUP QUESTIONS

1. Open in prayer.

2. Discuss: In chapter 9, the author presents a case for forming a band of brothers. Apart from this group, are there men in your life that you can speak to about life events and spiritual matters? Did you develop an individual improvement plan? Did it work? If you are willing, please share it with the group.

3. Read the story about Joshua Lawrence Chamberlain at the beginning of chapter 10.

4. Discuss: What do you think of this story? When down on your luck (so to speak), have you ever been treated with dignity and given an opportunity, like the mutineers were with Chamberlain? What was the result? Have you made any important decisions after reading *Words and Deeds* and participating in this small group study? Please share them with the group.

5. Read Mark 2:14, 9:35, and 16:15.

6. Discuss: What is the context? What are your observations? What is the true meaning of these passages? What is their application?

7. Discuss: What does it mean to be a follower of Christ? Can you be a Christian and still have your life look like that of your neighbor who takes no interest in God? Do we have freedom in Christ to do or say whatever we want? Are there any limits? What does it mean to be "all in"? What does it mean to disciple others? Are we doing a good job of this in Christianity today?

8. Pre-work: Ask if anyone would like to share what they wrote down for questions 1–4 in the Individual Journal Questions section. With question 4, would anyone be willing to share with the group which issues they circled? Please remind everyone that what is shared in the group *stays in the group*, and work together to hold each other accountable for the issues shared man to man.

9. Teamwork: How can each individual participating in this study help his "team" accomplish the mission of being a disciple and discipling others?

10. Cross-thought (if time allows): Read Luke 9:57-62. What is the meaning of Jesus' words in verse 62? How does it relate to us when we struggle with our faith?

11. Close in prayer after asking if anyone else has something to share with the group.

COLLECTIVE THOUGHTS

Our God is a God who invites us into a relationship with Him. In Scripture, it is described as being invited to a banquet or feast. With this invitation, Jesus calls men to repent, to break away from evil works that are ruining their lives. It is a summons for men to turn *away from* sin and turn *to*

God. This summons is also an announcement that God is doing something great, and if men repent of their sins and follow Christ, then they will be blessed—in this life and the life to come.

THE SCOUT

POSITIVES

+ Coolness/calmness

+ Maintains composure (S)

+ Team builder (T)

+ Quiet loyalist

+ Behind-the-scenes worker

NEGATIVES

- Can miss opportunities

- May be perceived as non-engaging (R)

- Unable to communicate deep feelings

- Expects people to read his mind (L)

THE STATESMAN

POSITIVES

+ Loyal and true (R)

+ Enthusiastic

+ Keeps perspective (S)

+ Has conviction

+ Team leader (T)

+ Has integrity

+ Active, trusts workers, leads by example, and makes good decisions (L)

THE SENTRY

POSITIVES

+ Takes life as it comes

+ Not worried about appearances

+ Satisfied with simplicity

NEGATIVES

- Every man for himself (R)

- Buries issues; others out to get him (S)

- Team irritant (T)

- Passive; too apathetic to create lasting change (L)

THE SALESMAN

POSITIVES

+ Outgoing and friendly (R)

+ Makes deals

+ Team spokesman (T)

+ Life of the party

+ Makes others feel at ease

NEGATIVES

- Erratic and impulsive (S)

- Can be a wolf in sheepskin

- My way or the highway (L)

- Deals are self-focused

- Perceived shallowness

AREAS OF LIFE

R: Relationships; S: Stress; T: Teamwork; L: Leadership

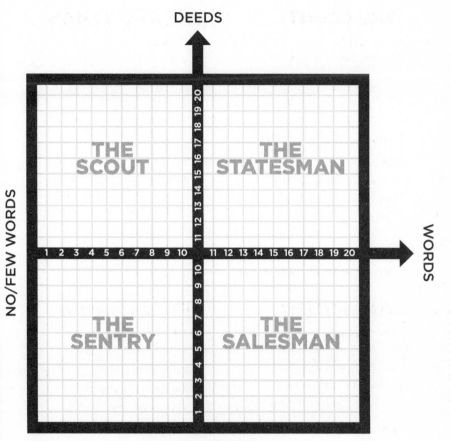

KEY POINTS TO PLOT

▲ - Where others see you

● - Where you see yourself

★ - Where you want to be

ACKNOWLEDGMENTS

Men who helped with the discussion guide or diagnostic concept include Scott Bonney, Alan Cole, Mike DuCharme, Scott Hagen, Major General Tom S. Jones (USMC), Tony Miltenberger, Craig Pache, Steve Yarber, and Tim Goeglein, who spoke to me about the dangers of pride (including his rise and fall in the George W. Bush White House). I thank *The Lion and the Lamb* editor Vicki Zimmer, who also helped with *Words and Deeds* in its early form. I thank my friend and agent, Dan Balow, from the Steve Laube Agency. I thank the NavPress and Tyndale House publishing teams for making this work a reality, especially Don Pape and David Zimmerman. NavPress introduced me to Jim Downing—an early Navigator and war hero from Pearl Harbor—who mentored me during the final year this book was written.

I thank my incredible wife, Lauri, a constant encourager and words and deeds woman. I also thank my children, Nickolas, Madison, Hannah, and Isaiah, who helped me with an early version of the survey, along with my siblings, Calvin Causey, Carol Mahan, and Nat Causey. Nat's men's ministry at the Westminster Presbyterian Church in Huntsville, Alabama, contributed toward the diagnostic research, along with several other men's groups, including Henry Foster's "The Climb Studio" group in Columbia, South Carolina; Scott Abrams's men's accountability group in Willmar, Minnesota; Dale Brynestad's men's group and son Chris, in Corpus Christi, Texas; Nick's cadet company at the United States Military Academy at West Point, New York; Chris Heaton's and Alan Cole's men's ministry at Crossway Fellowship in Manassas, Virginia; and Cabot Ashwill's men's group at LifeSpring Community Church in Spring Grove, Illinois.

Last, I thank three army organizations: the US Army Chaplain Center and School, who allowed the 2016 AIT class of 56Ms to participate with the diagnostic tool; the US Army Research Institute for the Behavioral and Social Sciences at Fort Belvoir, Virginia, for their time teaching me about variables rendering an effective survey; and the US Army Chaplain Corps Museum at Fort Jackson, South Carolina, including the museum director, Marcia McManus, who opened up the museum archives and allowed me to study ship manifest records and sworn affidavits of the *Dorchester* survivors.

Three words from Scripture banged around in my head while writing *Words and Deeds*. Though not placed together in a specific text, they are there, present when Jesus explains the greatest commandment; when Paul writes the Corinthians about the noblest gift; and when John's letter details the marks of a true believer. The three words—"nothing without love"—are not only true of us in this lifetime but also in the memories of us afterward. "They will remember how much you loved them, not much else," I was warned when entering ministry. So true. Our love echoes all around us, and the people listed above demonstrate that well.

NOTES

INTRODUCTION
1. *The Papers of Dwight David Eisenhower: The War Years*, vol. 3 (Baltimore: Johns Hopkins Press, 1970), 1913.

CHAPTER 1: THE MAN IN THE ARENA
1. This story is retold with permission from the US Army Chaplain Corps Museum at Fort Jackson, SC. Museum director Marcia McManus allowed me to review historical pages from the National Archives and ship manifest records and to study the sworn affidavits of the survivors.
2. Also written as Kengal Linawauel on official Department of the Navy correspondence of those rescued from the *Dorchester*.
3. "Actions speak louder than words" (Anonymous). "'Tis a kind of good deed, to say well: and yet words are no deeds" (William Shakespeare). "The chief difference between words and deeds is that words are always intended for men for their approbation, but deeds can be done only for God" (Leo Tolstoy). "Deeds, not words shall speak me" (John Fletcher). "Whoever said the pen is mightier than the sword obviously never encountered automatic weapons" (General Douglas MacArthur).
4. This nursery rhyme can be found in multiple locations; here is one of them: http://www.rhymes.org.uk/a4-a-man-of-words.htm.
5. This is an excerpt of a speech Theodore Roosevelt gave called "Citizenship In a Republic," delivered at the Sorbonne in Paris, France, on April 23, 1910. See Theodore Roosevelt, "Man in the Arena," April 23, 1910, Theodore Roosevelt Association, accessed November 15, 2017, http://www.theodoreroosevelt.org/site/c.elKSIdOWIiJ8H/b.9274065/k.8422/Man_in_the_Arena.htm.

6. Barna Group, "10 Facts about America's Churchless," December 10, 2014, https://www.barna.com/research/10-facts-about-americas-churchless/.
7. The cult leader's name was Jim Jones, of the 1978 Jonestown, Guyana, tragedy.
8. The account of Washington's prayer is hard to verify. The original manuscript of Snowden's diary is at the Historical Society of Pennsylvania, call number PHi.Am 1561–1568. You can read about this episode at http://www.ushistory.org/valleyforge/washington/prayer.html.

CHAPTER 2: INTEGRITY DEFINED

1. General Douglas MacArthur's "I Have Returned" speech, delivered via radio message from a portable radio set at Leyte, Philippines, October 20, 1944. See Douglas MacArthur, "To the People of the Philippines, Oct. 20, 1944," VCRT MacArthur Forum, accessed November 15, 2017, http://www.macarthurmilwaukeeforum.com/resources/speech-to-the -people-of-the-phillipines/.
2. Jonah Goldberg, "Empty Integrity," *National Review*, November 17, 2014.
3. *The Wire*, season 4, episode 7, "Unto Others," directed by Anthony Hemingway, written by David Simon et al., aired October 29, 2006, on HBO, https://www.hbo.com/the-wire.
4. C. S. Lewis, *Mere Christianity* (New York: MacMillan, 1952), 19.
5. The Lockman Foundation, *The New American Standard Exhaustive Concordance of the Bible* (Nashville: Holman Bible Publishers, 1981), s.v. "integrity."
6. Douglas MacArthur, *Revitalizing a Nation: A Statement of Beliefs, Opinions, and Policies Embodied in the Public Pronouncements of General of the Army Douglas MacArthur* (Chicago: Heritage Foundation, 1952), 28.

CHAPTER 3: AN HONEST ASSESSMENT OF SELF

1. These words are from an article passed around the Pentagon entitled "The Gun Doctor," written by B. J. Armstrong, January 27, 2015.
2. Fyodor Dostoyevsky, *The Brothers Karamazov*, trans. Constance Garnett (Overland Park, KS: Digireads.com Publishing, 2017), 35.

CHAPTER 4: THE SENTRY AND THE SALESMAN

1. William Shakespeare, *Macbeth*, ed. C. W. Crook (London: Ralph, Holland & Co., 1906), 94.

CHAPTER 5: THE SCOUT AND THE STATESMAN

1. President Ronald Reagan, on January 28, 1986, declared, "For the families of the seven, we cannot bear, as you do, the full impact of this tragedy. But we feel the loss, and we're thinking about you so very much. Your

loved ones were daring and brave, and they had that special grace, that special spirit that says, 'Give me a challenge, and I'll meet it with joy.'" Ronald Reagan, address to the nation on the explosion of the space shuttle *Challenger*, January 28, 1986, http://www.presidency.ucsb.edu /ws/?pid=37646.

2. "Eisenhower and the Little Rock Crisis," America's Story from America's Library, accessed January 29, 2018, http://www.americaslibrary.gov /aa/eisenhower/aa_eisenhower_littlerock_1.html.

CHAPTER 7: THE GAP

1. Pride is so insidious that it can manifest itself even within servanthood, suffering, and humility. For instance, the moment a man pauses to reflect on his suffering and compares it to another man's suffering, pride wrestles inside his heart and places his focus back on himself.

2. Walter Hooper, ed., *The Collected Letters of C. S. Lewis* (New York: HarperSanFrancisco, 2004), 2:122.

3. *Collected Letters of C. S. Lewis*, 123.

4. Carl P. E. Springer, *Luther's Aesop* (Kirksville, MO: Truman State University Press, 2011), 124.

CHAPTER 8: FORCE MULTIPLIERS

1. *Saving Private Ryan*, directed by Steven Spielberg (Universal City, CA: Dreamworks, 1999), DVD.

2. Mike Santangelo and David Krajicek, "Officer Steven McDonald Paralyzed from Central Park Shooting in 1986," *Daily News*, January 10, 2017, http://www.nydailynews.com/new-york/nyc-crime/steven -mcdonald-paralyzed-central-park-shooting-1986-article-1.2942841.

3. In our marriage book *UnBreakable*, Tony Miltenberger and I teach a tool called CAM, the Communication Acceleration Method. The premise is that when someone is talking, we listen and repeat back to them what they said, so they know we have heard them, *even if we disagree*. The response begins with "So, what you're saying is . . ." This simple tool has helped couples, because when a spouse feels listened to, it gives her the gift of presence.

4. Promptness is not a particularly prominent biblical value: Jesus was deliberately late in visiting Lazarus, for example, and Saul was confronted by Samuel for not waiting for Samuel before offering a sacrifice. However, Scripture *does* speak to being diligent and courteous, and it says that we should honor others. A little effort in something as small as promptness can bring great rewards and is a force multiplier because it can earn trust.

5. Francis Brown, *The Brown-Driver-Briggs Hebrew and English Lexicon* (Peabody, MA: Hendrickson, 1996), 336.

6. Walter Bauer and Frederick William Danker, *A Greek-English Lexicon of the New Testament and other Christian Literature* (Chicago: University of Chicago Press, 1979), 5.

CHAPTER 9: YOU AS STATESMAN

1. Martin Luther King Jr., "Letter from a Birmingham Jail," https://www.africa.upenn.edu/Articles_Gen/Letter_Birmingham.html.

2. About five years ago I called up four friends (from different churches) who lived in the area and asked if they would like to meet regularly for prayer, Bible study, and accountability. Nearly every one of them told me they had recently been feeling the need for greater spiritual connection and deeper male friendships. The group lasted for two years (until I moved).

CHAPTER 10: THE DECISION

1. Joshua Lawrence Chamberlain, quoted in Phil Dourado, "The Speech that Changed the Course of the US Civil War," April 12, 2012, http://vault.theleadershiphub.com/blogs/speech-changed-course-us -civil-war. Edited for readibility.

2. "Andrew Tozier, Little Round Top and the Congressional Medal of Honor," American Civil War Forum, accessed January 29, 2018, americancivilwarforum.com/Andrew-tozier-little-round-top-and -the-congressional-medal-of-honor-126082.html.

3. Jacob (Genesis 32), Samson (Judges 16), David (1 Samuel 23–24), Rehoboam (1 Kings 12), Daniel (Daniel 6), Joseph (Matthew 1), Peter (Luke 5), the rich young ruler (Luke 18), Pilate (Luke 23), Paul (Acts 9).

A SIX-WEEK BIBLE STUDY GUIDE FOR SMALL GROUPS

1. "Messianic Secret," Oxford Biblical Studies Online, http://www.oxfordbiblicalstudies.com/article/opr/t94/e1244.

2. Josh McDowell, *More than a Carpenter* (Carol Stream, IL: Tyndale House Publishers, 1977), 57.

THE NAVIGATORS® STORY

———— ⬤ ————

T HANK YOU for picking up this NavPress book! I hope it has been a blessing to you.

NavPress is a ministry of The Navigators. The Navigators began in the 1930s when a young California lumberyard worker named Dawson Trotman was impacted by basic discipleship principles and felt called to teach those principles to others. He saw this mission as an echo of 2 Timothy 2:2: "And the things you have heard me say in the presence of many witnesses entrust to reliable people who will also be qualified to teach others" (NIV).

In 1933, Trotman and his friends began discipling members of the US Navy. By the end of World War II, thousands of men on ships and bases around the world were learning the principles of spiritual multiplication by the person-to-person teaching of God's Word.

After World War II, The Navigators expanded its ministry to include college campuses; local churches; the Glen Eyrie Conference Center and Eagle Lake Camps in Colorado Springs, Colorado; and neighborhood and citywide initiatives across the country and around the world.

Today, with more than 2,600 US staff members—and local ministries in more than 100 countries—The Navigators continue the process of making disciples who make more disciples, advancing the Kingdom of God in a world that desperately needs the hope and salvation of Jesus Christ and the encouragement to grow deeper in relationship with Him.

NAVPRESS was created in 1975 to advance the calling of The Navigators by bringing biblically rooted and culturally relevant products to people who want to know and love Christ more deeply. In January 2014, NavPress entered into an alliance with Tyndale House Publishers to strengthen and better position our rich content for the future. Through *The Message* Bible and other resources, NavPress seeks to bring positive spiritual movement to people's lives.

If you're interested in learning more or becoming involved with The Navigators, go to www.navigators.org. For more discipleship content from The Navigators and NavPress authors, visit www.thedisciplemaker.org. May God bless you in your walk with Him!

Sincerely,

DON PAPE
VP/PUBLISHER, NAVPRESS

www.navpress.com

CP1308